Y0-AWG-442

REPTILES
ROUND THE WORLD

NEW YORK

Alfred A. Knopf

REPTILES
Round the World

A Simplified Natural History

OF THE

Snakes, Lizards, Turtles,
& Crocodilians

BY

CLIFFORD H. POPE

Illustrated by Helen Damrosch Tee-Van

THIS IS A BORZOI BOOK, PUBLISHED BY ALFRED A. KNOPF, INC.

This title was originally catalogued by the Library of Congress as follows:

598 Pope, Clifford Hillhouse   Reptiles around the world; a simplified natural history of the snakes, lizards, turtles and crocodilians. Illustrated by Helen Damrosch Tee-Van.

1. Reptiles.

L.C. Catalog Card Number: 57-9198   ISBN: 0-394-91539-9 (Lib. ed.)

3/81

TO
My Wife

Acknowledgments

INDEBTEDNESS to my wife, Sarah H. Pope, is beyond measure. She has spent nearly as much time as I, helping with all but the general plan and actual writing of this book. Her name is not with mine on the title page merely because she steadfastly refused to have it there.

Helen Tee-Van drew all the illustrations. I am grateful for her sympathetic interest, as well as for her care in gathering material and in making layouts. Her patience in deciphering written directions and her willingness to make changes were remarkable. Dr. James A. Oliver, Curator of Reptiles, New York Zoological Society, read the entire manuscript and suggested many improvements. He also helped immeasurably with the illustrating by giving advice and criticism, supplying literature, and by making living reptiles available for portrait studies. Dr. Oliver's generosity with his knowledge, his time, and his material is deeply appreciated. Publications of the New York Zoological Society have been invaluable source material for illustration. Dr. Arnold A. Zimmermann of Northfield offered constructive criticism of illustration layouts and helped in other ways. Mrs. Edgar Andrew Collard of Montreal, Canada, supplied information on the growth of her pet cooter.

The illustrated account of the life of the collared lizard is based on *An Ecological Study of the Collared Lizard (Crotaphytus collaris)*, University of Kansas Publications, Museum of Natural History, Vol. 8 (1956), pp. 213–274. No one has ever made better life history studies of lizards than has Dr. Henry S. Fitch, author of this work.

Contents

List of Illustrations

Introduction

MAN *has been fascinated by other animals for tens of thousands of years. This is proved by superb paintings such as those made some twenty thousand years ago on walls of the Cave of Lascaux, near Montignac, France. The domestication of many kinds of animals is further evidence of man's intense interest in them. In spite of this, it was not until the beginning of the Christian era, or a little earlier, that the Greeks and the Chinese attempted to study objectively all the animals known to them. The Greek attempts, so familiar to us, and those of the Chinese, just now coming to light, seem crude in comparison with modern efforts. This is because, during the last two centuries, new methods of investigation have completely revolutionized the study of animal life. Greek and Chinese zoology now stand in relation to modern zoology much as, in transportation, an ox cart stands to a jet plane. By reading this book you can learn more about reptiles than the greatest Greek or Chinese scholar could ever have learned.*

The study of reptiles and amphibians (herpetology to the initiated) is a small but rapidly growing branch of zoology. During the last few decades, the United States has become the center of this study. Europe has taken second place, though it still leads the world in the use of reptiles and amphibians for casual observation in home aquaria and terraria. This interest is pursued in Europe much as the interest in tropical fishes is pursued in the United States. In the New World, Brazil rates second to the United States as a center of reptile study. Several Asiatic countries, especially China, India, Ceylon, Japan, and Israel, have also developed a serious interest in herpetology. The Union of South Africa leads Africa in this regard.

It was not long ago that a person in the United States deeply interested in snakes, let us say, was considered queer. Such is no longer the case. Several large universities of this country always have graduate students studying reptiles. There are literally thousands of people who pursue the study diligently, though less seriously, or keep living reptiles as a hobby. Two journals, Copeia and Herpetologica, publish short, technical papers on reptiles and amphibians; the latter publication is entirely herpetological. There is, however, no popular magazine of this nature.

This does not mean that in the United States a student of reptiles and amphibians, no matter how learned, can easily earn his support by use of herpetological knowledge alone. Nearly all the positions that would allow this can still be counted on the fingers of one hand, and a specialist who takes one of these is likely to keep it until his retirement. The great majority of herpetologists support themselves by teaching biology or zoology, or by working for zoos or in animal conservation. Then there are always a few amateurs who prefer to make a living in work entirely unrelated to zoology. Some of the greatest herpetologists have belonged to this group. Incidentally, though most herpetologists, professional and otherwise, are men, not a few women have distinguished themselves in this field. At present each of two of

*the largest national museums of the world has a woman as cura-
tor of amphibians and reptiles.*

*Before animals can be studied properly, they must be classified.
An animal without a name is like a kitchen pot without a handle.
As you can imagine, the classification of animals has by now become complicated. Fortunately, for our purpose, only a few basic
terms have to be understood. The two most important of these
are species (plural: species) and genus (plural: genera). By and
large, a "species" is to a scientist nothing more than a "kind"
to others, and a genus is a group of closely related species. For
example, among mammals, a lion is one species of cat, a tiger
another. These and other typical wild cats are classified as a
single genus (Felis). Less typical cats are placed in other genera, which together make up a family (Felidæ), all the cats.
Families are arranged into orders, orders into classes. All mammals constitute one class, all reptiles another. Domestic cats are,
of course, descendants of various species of wild cats more or less
mixed up by breeding under control of man.*

PART I
REPTILE LIFE

Introducing Reptiles

ALLIGATORS, true crocodiles, caimans, and gavials (all together known as crocodilians) are the giants of the reptile world. No crocodilian is small; the smallest one, which lives in Africa, grows to a length of three and three-quarters feet. The rest of the crocodilians, with two exceptions, are at least as long as a tall man is tall; the longest may measure as much as twenty-three feet. Can you imagine four tall men lying on the ground, the feet of one against the head of the next? This will give you an idea of how much space one of the longest of the crocodilians occupies.

Most people can see fully grown crocodilians only in a zoo, for not only are they large but also they are few in number. In the whole world only twenty-three species can be found, and of these, all but two live in hot tropical countries. One is the American alligator,* which can still be seen in some of the low, wild parts of our

*A list of common and technical names of species and genera in this book begins on page 189.

southeastern states. For every kind of crocodilian on this earth, there are hundreds of kinds of other reptiles, as you shall soon find out.

The old saying, "When you've seen one, you've seen them all," applies to crocodilians better than to any other reptiles. The only noticeable difference among crocodilians is in the shape of the head when observed from above. Some have broad snouts and some have narrow ones. The gavial, sometimes known as gharial, of East Pakistan and adjacent regions has a snout so long and slender that it is just about as deep as it is broad. Except for the many long teeth set in both jaws, the gavial's snout looks much like a round stick.

Let us consider another reptile group that is perhaps more familiar to most of us than the crocodilians—the turtles. All of us know how well a turtle is protected by its shell. On the other hand, few of us know that the shell makes it impossible for the turtle to breathe like other "higher" land animals. (By "higher" land animals we mean those having backbones.) Most backboned land animals draw air into their lungs by expanding the chest. The turtle has special muscles that draw air in without changing the size of the chest. These muscles are placed in back of the lungs; when expanded, the lungs press against the intestines causing them to take up less space. The turtle, then, did not get its shell without giving up something that all its relatives use to great advantage.

The next most interesting thing about a turtle is its lack of teeth. Here again it has departed from the ways of most other backboned animals and is more like a bird than a reptile. If you watch a tame turtle eat, you will see that it has no trouble holding and crushing food. This is because, instead of being set with teeth, the jaws are covered with hard stuff something like your finger-nails; the ridge of each jaw comes to a sharp edge. And if you look at enough different kinds of turtles you will see that, in some, part of the edges of the jaws are sharp projections that act like real teeth. The turtle has scored again: it eats well without true teeth just as it breathes well in spite of its rigid chest.

Turtles are found in as many parts of the earth as are any other reptiles. In spite of this, there are not as many different species of turtles as there are of snakes or lizards. You have already learned that crocodilians are very few in number, there being only twenty-three species. For every species of crocodilian, there are about ten species of turtles, making a total of two hundred and thirty turtle species. Multiply this by eleven and you get approximately the number of species of snakes as well as of lizards.

Certain turtles are often called "tortoises" or even "terrapins." In this book the general name turtle in-cludes *all* tortoises and terrapins. There are so many more kinds of turtles in this country than in Great Britain that the early settlers were confused and used the words "turtle" and "tortoise" carelessly. "Terrapin" was bor-rowed from the Indians. Some strictly land turtles are referred to as tortoises in pages that follow. Also, our salt-marsh turtle is called a terrapin (diamondback).

The crocodilians are famous for their size, the turtles for their shell, and the poor lizards, in this country at least, for nothing in particular. What is even worse, in

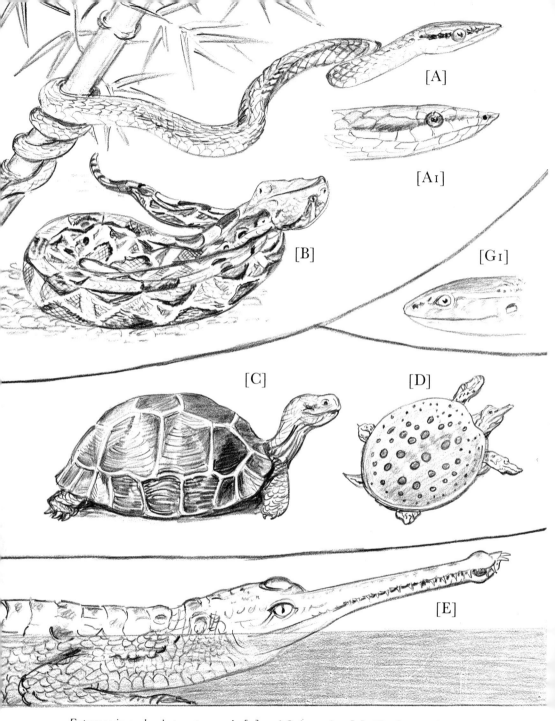

Extremes in snake shapes: tree snake [A] and Gaboon viper [B]. Turtles vary just as much: giant tortoise [C] and softshell turtle [D]. The gavial [E] has a snout of an extreme type; compare this snout with the American alligator's [I] shown opposite.

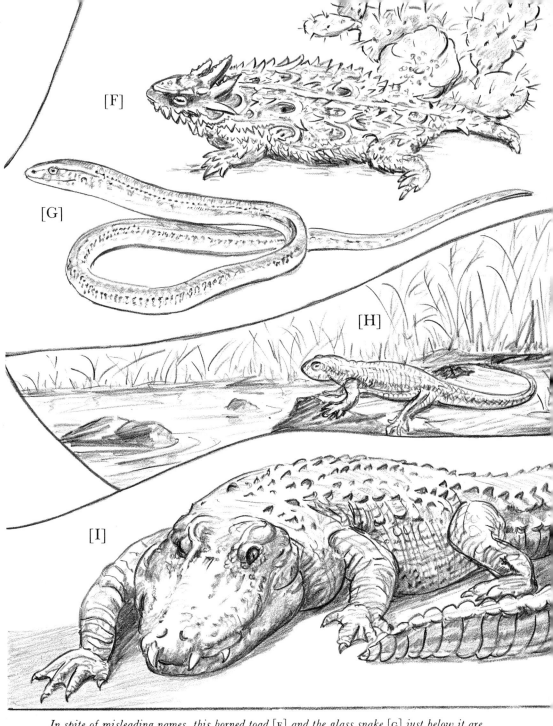

In spite of misleading names, this horned toad [F] *and the glass snake* [G] *just below it are both lizards. The ear of the glass snake (see its head* [G₁] *on opposite page) shows that it is not a snake;* no *snake has an ear-opening. The salamander* [H] *has no scales.*

the eastern half of the United States it is frequently almost impossible to distinguish lizards from salamanders because of their similar shapes. To tell them apart you have to look closely at the skin, which is scaly in lizards, scaleless in salamanders; dry in all lizards, moist in nearly all salamanders. If you remember that the salamander's skin must be *kept* moist or the poor thing will dry out quickly, you will be better able to distinguish between lizards and salamanders. If you find a creature that is basking in the sun or living in a hot, dry place, it is probably a lizard; if it is found in water or in a damp, cool place, it most likely is a salamander. From this you will also come to the correct conclusion that the dry Southwest is the home of most of our lizards, and the eastern forests, which are moist, the home of most of our salamanders. You should remember also that any animal called a "spring lizard" is really a salamander, and it is not hard to see how it got such a name. That moist skin of a salamander brings to mind a frog, and, indeed, the salamander is much more closely related to the frog than it is to any reptile.

Lizards make up the only group of backboned animals in which some have large, strong legs and others have no legs at all. Moreover, between these extremes there are all degrees: lizards with legs that are mere tokens, others with legs that are fairly useful, still others with only moderately useful legs, and so on. Hardest of all to believe is the existence of well-legged species whose closest relatives are legless or nearly so. Imagine that if you can! In the United States the reptiles commonly called "glass snakes" are fine examples of legless lizards.

Whereas lizards have experimented with various degrees of "leglessness," snakes have gone even further. The nearest thing to a leg possessed by any snake is a mere spur. Even this is so small that you have to look hard to find it. It is no help in getting about and few snakes have it.

One would expect that snakes, handicapped as they are by lack of legs, would eat small animals that are easy to handle or would even live on plants, which never try to get away. But no snake lives on plants, and most snakes catch, subdue, and devour in one piece relatively large animals rather than small ones. Obviously snakes must possess some rather astonishing characteristics not common to other creatures. First, their needlelike teeth, which slant toward the throat, grasp prey so firmly that it has small chance to pull itself free. Second, the snake's great length and its ability to wrap around and squeeze its prey give this reptile a decided advantage in overcoming larger animals. Also, jaws that can be spread wide apart and skin that stretches like rubber enable the snake to swallow prey of great size. Many snakes, it should be added, have a way of injecting venom into prey, and this makes the holding and overpowering unnecessary. Among other reptiles, only our North American Gila monster and its close cousin of Mexico kill their prey with venom.

All reptiles are vertebrates (backboned animals). With the exception of the tuatara, reptiles can be classified in one of four major groups known as crocodilians, turtles, lizards, and snakes. The lonesome tuatara, a "living fossil" found only on tiny islands of New Zealand, is very rare indeed. There are, in all, about five thousand five hundred species of reptiles alive today.

How do these five thousand five hundred species of reptiles fit into the whole animal kingdom? The other backboned animals (vertebrates) are the fishes, the amphibians (frogs, toads, salamanders, and the almost unknown cæcilians), the birds, and the mammals (often wrongly called simply "animals"). Man, of course, is a mammal. All of these vertebrates together, including the reptiles, number only about thirty-five thousand species, whereas the vast world of animals without backbones (known to science as invertebrates) is composed of well over a million species, more than half of them insects. You might call this a case of the tail wagging the dog, for, as you see, the backbone-less animals—the invertebrates—constitute almost the entire animal kingdom. However, we vertebrates—though clearly a minority— can console ourselves by claiming to have a monopoly on intelligence, and when we claim this there is nobody to contradict us!

Locomotion

ANIMALS in general have three ways of getting about: flying, swimming, and walking-running-crawling-hopping. It is an odd fact that our language, unlike many others, does not have one simple and common word for continuous forward motion on land. When it comes to flying, the reptiles alive today fall flat, taking that expression in both its meanings. The great flying reptiles of ages gone by did no more than leave a record in the rocks. In the Old World, the little lizards known as "flying dragons" do sail from tree to tree by means of two flaps of skin, one along either side, and a few snakes make long sailing leaps without the aid of such flaps. However, neither snake nor lizard can be said to fly, and the thought of turtle or crocodilian floating through the air is in itself very funny and makes us laugh.

Swimming is quite another matter, since reptiles are as good swimmers as they are poor fliers. Snakes and lizards take to water almost like ducks, and crocodilians are actually amphibious, which means that they are at home on land and in water alike. Many turtles live in water, and even the tortoises, with all their lumpy shape and clumsiness, manage to swim well enough. The only astonishing thing about reptile swimming is that the legs of those with flexible bodies are not used but kept folded against the side; the animal is sent forward by a lateral curving of body and tail.

Reptile locomotion on land cannot be treated as briefly as can swimming and movement through the air. The crocodilians, with their four strong legs, walk or run in the ordinary manner. For short distances they can make good speed. Turtles do not have anything unusual to offer; they are slow-moving just as tradition describes them. A few water turtles, however, are much livelier than the clumsy land turtles.

Among the lizards, we find many complicated types of land locomotion, due to the great variety of shapes that lizards have. Added to this are wide differences in habits. Lizards may live in the ground, on or near its surface, or above it in trees and bushes. Neither turtles nor crocodilians climb or burrow, except when digging a home or "den." Climbing lizards hold on with claws or with combined claws and pads. The surface of each pad is beset with countless hooks that are too small for our eyes to see. It is often thought that either "suction" or stickiness plays a part, but this belief is entirely wrong. Nearly all geckos (lizards living in the warmest parts of the earth) have toes with pads.

As we have noted, many lizards have no legs and many have legs that are too small to be really useful. These limbless or nearly limbless reptiles move by curving the body from side to side in a way that is much like the common type of snake crawling. There are two very interesting things about these lizards. They usually have very long tails, which they can use in locomotion, and they have never adopted the climbing methods utilized by many snakes.

We must not overlook those peculiar creatures known as "worm lizards," though they are not considered to be proper lizards by all specialists. These burrowers live in the ground and their movements resemble the movements of worms rather than reptiles. They have no difficulty crawling backward—something that lizards seldom, if ever, do.

A few lizards exhibit a minor locomotion specialty. I refer to running on the hind legs, or, if you want to be scientific, bipedal locomotion. Many of my friends say that lizards doing this remind them of dinosaurs, but to me it is the other way around. *Who* has seen a dinosaur run on its hind legs? I use the word "specialty" in this regard because the few lizards that can run with the body erect do so only for short distances and when in a great hurry.

I have saved the dessert for the last. Snake locomotion is not only beautiful to see but baffling to study. You can watch a snake crawl for a long time and still be unable to determine just how it does so. In fact, students of reptiles have only recently ironed out some of the important but confusing details.

Let's start our study by putting a slender but lively snake on loose sand. After it has crawled for a while, you will see that the most conspicuous part of the track is a series of slightly curved piles of sand. Let the snake crawl again and notice that a pile is raised by each curve; you can easily conclude that the snake is advancing by pushing against these piles, which rapidly grow bigger and bigger. Next, place the snake on a very smooth surface (slightly greased glass will do) and see that it makes its usual motions, but gets nowhere; there is nothing to push against. These experiments will give you an understanding only of the commonest type of snake crawling.

To see the caterpillar type of crawling, you must have a heavy-bodied instead of a slender snake, and it is not likely that you will be able to lay your hands on one. Moreover, even a heavy-bodied snake cannot always be persuaded to try to crawl in this leisurely way. The name "caterpillar type" is, of course, somewhat misleading, since the snake has no feet. But a snake using this type of locomotion does advance in a straight line, as a caterpillar does, and waves of motion do pass down its body. Of course, the track is straight instead of curved. If you are lucky enough to see such movement and watch closely, you will note that the snake is shifting groups of belly scales forward, first raising them slightly before putting them down again. The waves move from the front toward the rear of the body in such smooth and uniform fashion that they seem to flow along, and the snake appears to do so, too.

It was long thought that the ribs, a pair for each belly scale, were being moved inside something like legs; the snake was described as "walking" on the ends of its ribs. It is now known that the ribs take no part, nor do the edges of the belly scales catch on the ground; the snake

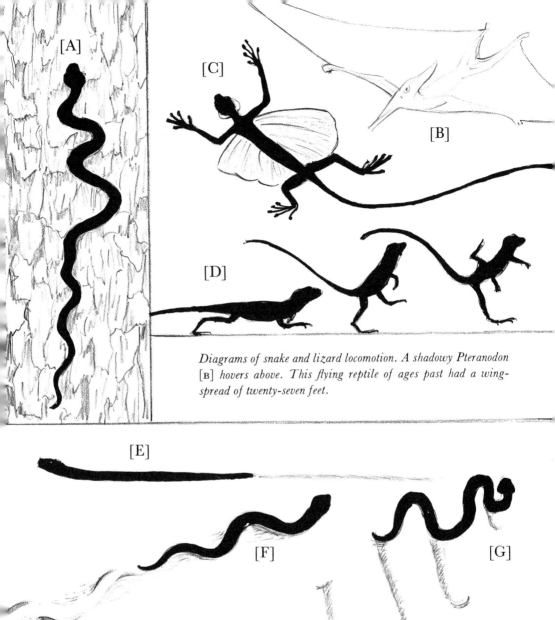

Diagrams of snake and lizard locomotion. A shadowy Pteranodon [B] *hovers above. This flying reptile of ages past had a wing-spread of twenty-seven feet.*

Snake climbing tree [A]. *Pteranodon* [B]. *Flying dragon* [C]. *Collared lizard running* [D]. *Caterpillar type of snake locomotion* [E]. *Usual type of snake locomotion* [F]. *Side-winding type of snake locomotion* [G].

is depending chiefly on friction between scales and ground. Caterpillar locomotion works even on sand because there is slight backward thrust. Little speed can be made, however, and snakes in a hurry nearly always fall back on the more common type of snake crawling described earlier.

If you watch a hurrying desert snake, preferably the sidewinder (a rattlesnake), you will be puzzled to see it move at an angle to the way you feel it should, and leave a track that is not continuous. It is almost rolling along. This "sidewinding" is especially suited to progress in loose sand.

Bushy growth and forests of tropical regions often contain plenty of snakes. This suggests that many snakes are excellent climbers. Though almost every snake climbs well enough, the specialist of these wooded regions has its own distinctive shape. Along each side of its belly (which is largely flat) there extends an angular ridge. This ridge is caused by a bend near the end of each scale that lies across the belly. These climbers have, then, a belly with two parallel ridges. The ridges, being sharp enough to catch on twigs and bark, greatly aid in climbing. A tree snake has little trouble going straight up the side of a vertical trunk unless the bark is very smooth. A climbing snake rarely wraps itself about trunk or branch like ribbon around a Maypole: it may do so occasionally when a *very* slender trunk, branch, or vine is being climbed. See the illustration on page 149 in the chapter that deals with South America.

Eating

EATING is something that every one of us has to do every day. Most of us enjoy it—so the subject is of great interest. As for the eating habits of reptiles, that can be a very interesting subject too!

It is easy to remember, in general, what reptiles feed on, if you realize that the groups are evenly divided in this respect. The crocodilians and snakes are animal-eaters, whereas the turtles and lizards eat *both* plants and animals. In scientific terms: the former groups are *carnivorous*, the latter groups, *omnivorous*.

The crocodilians have perhaps the most exciting eating habits—not only are they the largest reptiles, but also this group includes the only reptiles that eat us! We are happy to be able to report, however, that few of them ever devour human beings, and these few are to be found in parts of the world far removed from our United States.

The crocodilian's method of overcoming large prey is

unique. The victim is literally twisted apart until the pieces are small enough to be swallowed. After getting a firm grip, the powerful creature whirls over and over on its long axis. A leg or head is thus torn off and, if suitable in size, tossed by the jaws into a convenient position for swallowing. Tossing is necessary because the crocodilian tongue can only be raised and lowered, not moved forward and backward like yours. Chewing is something the crocodilian does not bother to do.

Anyone who recalls that certain crocodilians have very slender snouts might doubt that they could twist very well. Such a doubt is well founded. Have you ever tried to twist anything with a pair of slender tweezers? These slender snouts are really fish catchers; all the crocodilians that have them eat fishes. Presumably very large fishes would not be tackled, although there is little information on this point.

It has already been stated that all turtles lack real teeth. One thing is certain—they are never bothered with toothache, nor would they ever have any use for toothpicks. The edges of the turtle's jaws are not able to deal with hard or fibrous plants, so the food of the plant-eaters is limited to tender parts. In contrast to this, some of the kinds that eat animals have very strong jaws as well as special flat or ridged places in the mouth. These enable the jaws to crush snails and other shelled animals. Many species eat both animals and plants.

One bad result of being shut in by a shell is that when you get fat you cannot expand in all directions. Turtles are given to overeating, and those normally able to close themselves up completely may suffer from being too fat.

When they close the front part of the shell to protect head and front legs, the tail and hind legs stick out, and vice versa. Our box turtles are a good example.

As if to make up for the relatively uninteresting eating habits of most turtles, the alligator snapping turtle, a giant fresh-water kind, uses a clever trick. On the floor of its mouth there is a raised area that can be moved so that, to a fish at least, it suggests food. The structure is usually described as the turtle's "worm"; it is more accurately called a lure. Anyway, the alligator snapper, while lying on the bottom of lake or river, often opens the mouth and catches fishes by means of the lure. In very young turtles it is actually red, and looks a lot like a wiggling worm, as I have seen; in older turtles the lure seems to lose its color.

Lizards in general eat much like other vertebrates. Their tongues are especially interesting. On the one reptile extreme, crocodilians get along with a tongue that cannot be stuck out; on the other, the vast majority of snakes have the familiar forked tongue so often, but falsely, called a "stinger." Lizards go in for variety: tongues shaped like our own; tongues like ours but nicked just a bit at the tip; broad tongues deeply nicked; long forked tongues just like the tongue of a snake. The surface of the tongue may be scaled, ridged, or covered with little bumps. To cinch the matter, the true chameleons have developed the tongue to end all tongues! Its bulbous, sticky tip can be shot to a distance much greater than the length of head and body, and at a speed too fast for the eye to follow. Its action can be roughly likened to that of a boy's fingers popping fresh watermelon seeds. Some species of lizards eat plants as well as animals.

Among reptiles, the snake has the most remarkable eating habits. As these are closely tied up with structure, I brought out some important points in the first chapter. I shall begin here, just as the snake begins, with the finding of food. That lively forked tongue, instead of being a "stinger," is used in the trailing of prey; the tongue first picks up minute particles that hold the scent of the prey and then transfers these to little cavities in the front part of the roof of the mouth. There the particles are smelled, since the cavities are lined with a membrane that is really a smeller. The nose also smells, but divides the ability to do so with those cavities. If you drag a fish across a table, and then remove it and place a tame, fish-eating snake there, you will, with luck, see attempts to trail the scent.

After the victim is caught, it may, if very small, be swallowed at once; if larger, it may be overpowered by sheer weight; if very large, and the snake is a constricting kind, it will certainly be constricted. Many are the tales about the great power of large snakes; how they "crush every bone" in the victim's body. The truth is that, though reasonably strong, even the largest snakes do little or no crushing. Most victims will be animals that breathe by expanding the chest; the snake has only to get a snug grip with a few coils and, at each emptying of the victim's lungs, take up all the slack in these coils. The prey will soon suffocate without the cracking of a single bone. There will be nothing left for the snake to do but swallow the now helpless creature.

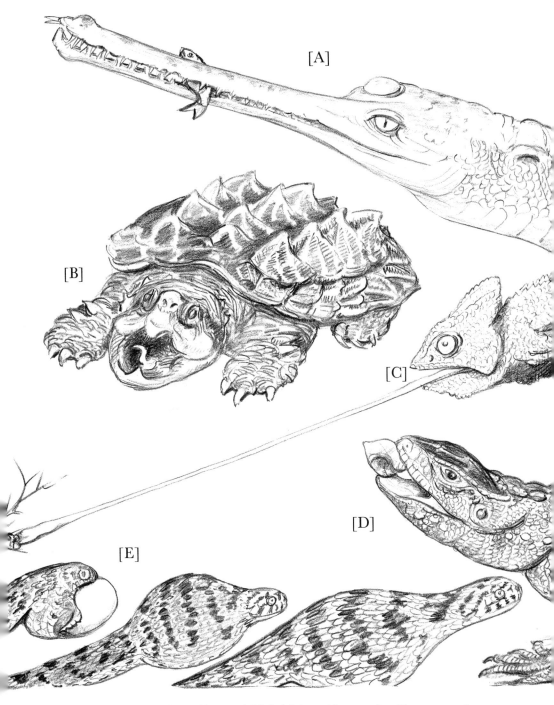

Reptiles with unusual eating habits: gavial [A] (*fish-catching snout*), *alligator snapping turtle* [B] (*lure*), *true chameleon* [C] (*popping tongue*), *caiman lizard* [D] *with snail, and famous egg-eating snake* [E] *with egg.*

The highly venomous snakes do not, of course, have to bother with such crude exertion. Since the venom is a specialized saliva, digestion of the prey starts at the minute of injection. Think of being slightly digested even before being swallowed!

The backward-slanting teeth of a snake grip so well that should the creature change its mind it may have trouble letting go. As a substitute for limbs such teeth are excellent, but for chewing they are useless. The snake must swallow things whole, and its fondness for large prey forces it to do considerable stretching. The halves of the lower jaw are attached to each other and to the rest of the skull in a way that allows them to move independently. Even each half of the upper jaw can be advanced by itself. All this jaw freedom allows the snake to pull itself over its food by getting one of its several half-jaws free and then shifting it forward to take a new grip. The process is repeated with the other half-jaws until the food has passed the head on its way down. After that, throat and body muscles take over until the stomach has received at least the forward end. I say "forward" because a snake often has to let part of a meal lie for a time in the gullet, or even stick out of the mouth. All this adds up to two very interesting facts: a snake thinks nothing of devouring something equal to itself in volume, and a snake can take in enough food at one time to supply its needs for weeks. Any snake in good condition can fast for a year.

Reproducing

PROBABLY the most important thing any animal does is to reproduce its kind; animals that have failed as a group to do so simply are not with us any more. In the higher animals there are two sexes, male and female. Reproduction depends on the union of two special types of cells, one from the female, the ovum, the other from the male, the sperm. To understand reproduction we must know how this union comes about, how the fertilized ovum develops, and how the young are brought into the world and cared for.

Among the higher animals reproduction shows a definite trend. We might say that at one extreme reproduction is casual and gross, at the other, careful and individual. A female fish may eject thousands of ova into the water and leave them to unite as best they can with sperm likewise ejected by the male. At the other extreme stands the human being with marriage, single births, and at least fifteen years of care by father and mother.

The progress from one of these extremes to the other

took millions of years, and was not made entirely by any one major group of animals. The reptiles are responsible for certain important steps. Their reproduction is interesting also because of the variety of different methods they have tried.

There are for us three important factors in typical fish reproduction: first, the necessity of a great deal of water; second, the union of ovum and sperm outside the bodies of the parents; and third, the waste involved, as a great number of cells are always lost.

Everyone knows that reptiles freed themselves from life in water, but few realize that in doing so they had a reproductive hurdle before them: the development of an egg so well protected that it could resist drying if laid on land. The reptiles made this hurdle and thus advanced beyond the stage of the amphibians (frogs, salamanders, and their kin) which had almost freed themselves from water, *except for reproduction*. So often one thing depends upon another. The protection for the united reproductive cells had to come from one of the parents, and the female was elected by Nature to provide it. Well protected from drying, however, a single cell would have no way of uniting with another. The whole problem was solved by bringing together ovum and sperm within the body of the female before the addition of any protection. This is known as internal fertilization, and the reptiles, I repeat, were first to place full reliance on it. As a little thought will convince anyone, internal fertilization helped to take care of the matter of waste in reproductive cells.

The variety in reptile reproduction mentioned above

calls for a little attention. This variety centers around the site of the growth of the embryo and its connection with the mother. The reptiles, speaking figuratively, could not decide whether to have the embryo grow in an egg or in the body of the female; if in the mother's body, whether to provide nourishment directly (through a placenta) as the mammal does. As a result, we find many reptiles that lay eggs and many that do not, and a fair number with a placenta not unlike that of the mammal. In sharp contrast stand the birds, which always lay eggs, and, the mammals, which give birth to their young in the same manner as humans. Of course, humans are mammals, too!

Enough of these broad generalizations; let us now see how each major group handles the important matter of reproducing its kind. The first step is always the getting together of male and female. Even this is not left to chance; one makes an effort to find the other at the proper time; then comes some form of courtship. In the American alligator, for example, the male, roaring loudly, strikes poses with neck region arched and tail waving. He finally seizes the back of his mate's neck in his great jaws. This may seem like cruel treatment, but you must remember that her back is well protected by scaly skin reinforced with bits of bone; she is literally a "roughneck."

As far as we know, all crocodilians lay eggs in nests that are in a few species made with considerable care. In these the female may remain on guard to defend her nest. This is uncommon enough among reptiles, but the crowning touch is the use of sound in releasing the offspring; when they grunt just after hatching, the female opens the nest to release them. No other reptile carries parental care even this far or makes use of sound in communicating with its young.

Unfortunately, the life histories of several of the crocodilians have not been worked out in detail and we still have to be guarded in the general statements that we make. The American alligator's habits are fairly well known, so I shall give a condensed account of nest building as performed by one female. Probably no other crocodilian surpasses this performance. The nest building by the American alligator is here divided into numbered steps for the sake of clarity.

First step: clearing an area about eight by ten feet in a brier patch by biting off, pulling up, and mashing down all the vegetation there. Second: making a pile of trash and fresh vegetation in the center of the cleared area by use of her mouth and backward movements of her body. Third: working this material into a well-packed, flat-topped mound by crawling over it and pulling the loose material toward the center. Fourth: making a hollow in the center of the mound by pushing her hind feet one at a time outward from the center, her front legs braced in the outer edge of the nest mass and her body slowly revolving about it. Fifth: filling the hollow with mouthfuls of mud and water plants taken from the bottom of the water near by. Sixth: smoothing and shaping the whole mound by moving around and around it and over its top. Seventh: making another hollow in the mound much as in step four. Eighth: depositing the eggs in the cavity, turning the body while doing so. Ninth: covering the eggs, first with the wet material taken from the nest rim with her mouth, and then with fresh mud and water plants from the water; pressing down and smoothing all this material with her belly while depositing it. Tenth: making the nest into a smooth-surfaced, cone-topped structure by crawling around and around on its slopes. This particular female worked off and on for three days and two nights.

In all the records of natural history it would be hard to find a more fascinating picture than this of the clumsy alligator making a nest with mud, trash, and fresh vegetation as material, her great belly and broad mouth as tools.

Courtship in turtles is varied. The giant tortoises violently pound their mates, using the body like a battering-ram, and utter resounding roars all the while. An unusual procedure is the waving or vibrating of the long fingernails of the male near or against the face of the female. This is seen in some water turtles of the United States, such as the painted turtle.

It was discovered not very long ago that some turtles lay eggs for years after one mating. This came as a great surprise. The belief had been that, among higher animals, a single mating produced but one clutch of eggs or brood of young. No reptile was included among the few exceptions. It is now known that certain snakes and a lizard are like turtles in this respect.

All turtles lay eggs, and these the female buries. Neither nest nor young is cared for by her. In fact, the female seems to have little idea just what is going on. A collector of sea-turtle eggs may sit behind her with a

bucket and take the eggs as they appear. The layer will
finally turn and cover up the nest just as thoroughly as
if it were full of eggs. The tears that she sheds have been
taken to be a sign of sorrow at loss of her eggs, but the
covering of the empty nest belies this. The crying is
nothing more than Nature's way of keeping turtle eyes
free of sand. The tears may begin to flow even before
she starts to dig.

This apparent unconcern of the laying turtle does not
mean that she cannot do a good job of nestmaking.
Chiefly with the hind flippers, sea turtles dig deep nests
in the sand, and in doing so show remarkable dexterity.
Only someone who has tried to do the same with the
hands will appreciate the skill shown by a turtle in making a neat hole in the sand as deep as the long flippers
will reach. Even the filling is done with great care, and
the site is packed down by the body. The leatherback so
thoroughly plows up the surrounding area that the nest,
which may be waist-deep to a man, can scarcely be
found. The size (half a ton and more) and strength of
this gigantic sandplow enable her to do a thorough job
of concealment. At the opposite extreme, some turtles
make simple nests or barely cover the eggs with debris.

The variety in reptile reproduction mentioned near
the beginning of this chapter and described a little
further on is not found in either turtles or crocodilians.
These remained conservative in sticking to the laying of
eggs. The snakes and lizards were the experimenters,
especially the snakes. Most books wrongly state that all
snakes reproduce by means of eggs, although in some
species the eggs are held in the body to hatch. It is time

The king cobra drags together material for her nest and then coils about her eggs.

The loggerhead leaves the waves, lays, buries her eggs, and returns to the sea.

A caiman guards her nest until the eggs hatch.

that this misleading statement was dropped. The truth is that most snakes do lay eggs, but a great many of them give birth much as do mammals. In the United States, for instance, there are about three egg-layers to two live-bearers. The young are born in a transparent membrane, from which they soon escape. Some of the species that give birth have a placenta, and through it the embryos get some direct nourishment. Such snakes are extremely near to mammals in method of reproducing.

The odd thing about this whole matter is that two species of snakes may be close cousins and yet differ as much in the method of reproduction as do mammals and birds. But even these snakes, so advanced in one way, did not ever develop parental care; the babies are fully prepared to take care of themselves. Certain egg-laying snakes coil about their eggs. Some female pythons develop a slight "fever" while doing this, and thus speed up the growth of the embryos.

Snake nests are very simple things. The large but crude nest constructed by the king cobra is the only one worthy of the name; the rest of the egg-laying snakes merely shape up a natural cavity in almost any soft material; earth, rotten wood, sawdust, old manure piles, or other debris of a more or less natural kind. Abandoned animal burrows, holes in ancient walls, and those left after the decay of stumps and roots may be used. Many females occasionally lay at the same general site, leaving scores or even hundreds of eggs near together.

Lizards, like snakes, are divided between those that give birth and those that lay eggs. The first method is widespread, but on the whole less so than among snakes. Lizards are seldom thought of as giving birth, although this method is common in at least one big family. Lizards select an interesting variety of nesting places. They may use the same kind of sites that snakes like, but not exclusively. They have a few noteworthy preferences of their own. For example, many geckos stick their eggs to vertical surfaces such as the bark of trees. The nests themselves are simple enough, perhaps even more so than snake nests. Many lizards guard their nests but none takes an interest in the young.

At the beginning of this chapter the trend from large to small numbers of offspring was pointed out. Since the reptiles lie in the middle of the vertebrate evolutionary line from the fishes through the mammals, it is interesting to make some comparisons. In round numbers, a pair of fishes may release in a year hundreds of thousands of ova and sperm, a pair of amphibians tens of thousands, a pair of reptiles may produce a few hundred young, and a pair of mammals or birds, about a score. These estimates stand for the big producers; the averages would be far lower, but no one knows them. The estimates merely serve to show the sharp downward trend as greater care is bestowed on the offspring. There is, of course, much more waste in the fishes and amphibians than in the rest. In mammals the waste is no doubt least of all. If it were anything comparable to that easily sustained by the fishes and amphibians, the mammals would simply disappear. To be more specific, we may state that the maximum number of young per birth for mammals is about twenty; few species exceed ten, and great numbers produce only one or two offspring at a time.

A comparison of the reptile groups is interesting. I shall refer only to the number of eggs or young produced at a time. The turtles take first prize with several species that exceed the hundred mark, and a maximum somewhere between two and three hundred. The other extreme is a single egg, although this is indeed an extreme, the vast majority of turtles laying at least several eggs at once. Snakes come next. The maximum figure for them is about a hundred, and the interesting thing here is that not only the largest but a few species of medium size approximate this number. Among the turtles the largest species are the biggest producers; at least the correlation seems to be closer. The lizards come last with a maximum a little less than half that for the snakes and only one-fifth or one-sixth that for the turtles. This is strange, to say the least. On the low extreme the lizards are the winners with great numbers of species that regularly lay just two eggs at a time, some only one. Obviously, the lizards have the lowest group average.

The crocodilians have been left out of this discussion because they stand apart for two reasons: the small number of species (twenty-three), and the fact that probably no species lays very small clutches of eggs. Information is far from complete, but it looks as though all of them lay clutches of fifteen or more eggs. Tentatively, the maximum may be put in the eighties; several species fall not very far short of this (fifty to sixty eggs). With no really small numbers to pull it down, the group average would no doubt stand higher than for any of the others.

Size

SIZE of animals fascinates all of us. Who has not bragged about catching the biggest fish or seeing the longest snake? There is so much talk of this kind that scientists tend to scoff, and underrate the importance of size. This is merely going to the other extreme, since size *is* of great importance in the relationships of wild animals.

I have already pointed out the lack of truly small crocodilians and the fact that the largest kinds may measure as much as twenty-three feet. These reptiles are the largest of all in average size; the giants among them surpass in weight all other reptiles except the huge leatherback turtle and, perhaps, very large marine log-gerheads. It is unfortunate that we have little information on the weight of gigantic individuals of the biggest kinds of crocodilians. Our own alligator is a chunky species and, at a length of twelve feet, it weighs about five hundred pounds. This is not much if compared with the fifteen or sixteen hundred pounds of the heaviest leatherback turtles. Crocodilians do not live in places where scales are handy, and the difficulties of weighing a chunky creature more than twenty feet long are considerable.

As just stated, the marine leatherback is the heaviest of all reptiles. Full-grown leatherbacks measure from

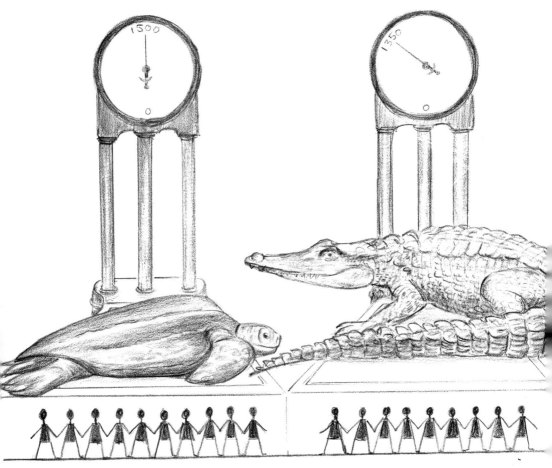

LEATHERBACK TURTLE
1500 pounds

AMERICAN CROCODILE
1350 pounds

The leatherback wins the gold medal in this all-reptile weight contest. It would

eight to twelve feet, flipper tip to flipper tip, and weigh
from one-half to three-fourths of a ton. The largest of
the hard-shelled sea turtles, the green and the loggerhead, sometimes reach a weight of only one or two hundred pounds less than half a ton. The biggest of land
turtles, the tortoises of remote islands (Galápagos and

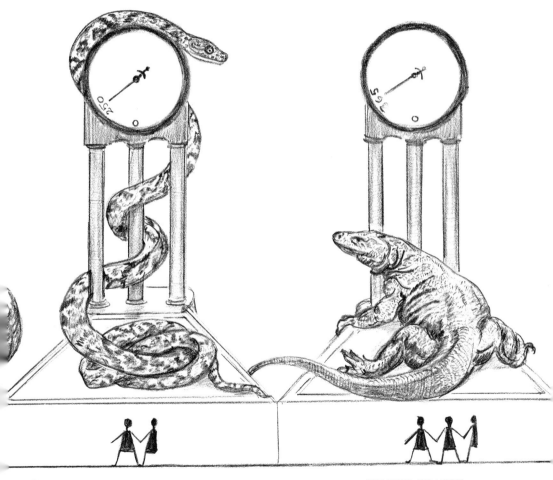

PYTHON
250 pounds

KOMODO DRAGON
365 pounds

take twenty-three or twenty-four average men to balance these four champions.

others) do not fall far behind; one has tipped the scales at five hundred and sixty pounds, and weights of from three to four hundred pounds are not uncommon.

At the other extreme, turtles distinguish themselves by including many small kinds. In the United States, where turtles abound, there are several species with an average length that falls between three and four inches. One of these, the bog turtle, is a good example; its average length is just three and a half inches. Since no turtle is slender, the weight of these midgets is many times greater than that of the smallest snakes and lizards.

LENGTH AND WEIGHT OF A SMALL TURTLE, LIZARD, AND SNAKE

	LENGTH (*inches*)	WEIGHT (*1 oz. = 28.4 g.*)
Yellow mud turtle (*Kinosternon*)	5.0	13.8 ounces
Dwarf spiny lizard (*Leposoma*)	3.6	1.0 gram
Yellow-faced worm-snake (*Leptotyphlops*)	6.3	1.4 grams

The turtle was measured from tip to tip of its upper shell, not following the curve. The snake and lizard were measured from tip of snout to end of tail.

Snakes really have two sizes: the actual tape-measure size, and the one registered on the alarmed human brain. A reliably truthful lad once led me to a spot where a snake had just escaped him. According to the boy, the length of the snake was tremendous. When we finally caught it, the snake apparently had dwindled to a more reasonable length! Its tape-measure length turned out to be considerably shorter than its reported length. The lad was highly embarrassed for fear of being thought a liar. Of course, he had only reported what his excited mind had registered. In describing snakes, the expressions, "as big as my arm" or "as big as my leg" have been used so much that they seldom have any truth in them. Perhaps the only way to get a tape-measure mind about snake lengths and girths is to become used to these reptiles.

Snake hides are often another source of mistakes about lengths. The skinning of a snake, even though done with great care, produces a hide noticeably longer than the snake was to begin with. For example, the hide of a python seven feet long will measure well over eight feet. Then there are merchants who like to trick tourists by artfully sewing together the hides of two snakes; only a careful search will disclose the seam. The final discouraging thing about snake dimensions is that measurements of gigantic individuals of the largest kinds are few and far between.

Enough of the difficulties; let us turn to the best knowledge we have. The reticulate python, an Asiatic reptile, is usually credited with the greatest size of any snake, and given a maximum length of thirty-two feet. The second in size, the anaconda, probably falls short of this by two or three feet. In all justice to this South American giant, persistent rumors of individuals approximating forty feet must be admitted. The big snake of Africa is the rock python, twenty-five feet long at most. Australia is not without its champion, the amethystine python, twenty-one feet. The boa constrictor, found in both North and South America, is rarely even fifteen feet long, and this in spite of the common belief that it is the biggest of all. A recent record puts the maximum length of this snake at eighteen and a half feet. We can rightly ask for confirmation of this. It is interesting that these huge species are so nicely spread over the world, every continent but Europe having a noteworthy one.

The lizards are the most disappointing of reptiles when it comes to size. There is but one gigantic species among them, the Komodo dragon, which may grow to be ten feet two inches long and weigh three hundred and sixty-five pounds. However, an individual eight feet two inches in length weighed only a hundred and sixty-three pounds. Certain other monitors rate next in size. The monitors frequent Africa, southern Asia, the East Indian Islands, Australia, and some of the islands of the Pacific Ocean. Oddly enough, there are species of monitors that never grow more than ten inches long. The largest of monitors may weigh thirty-seven hundred times as much as the smallest!

In addition to a host of truly small lizards there are a great many that measure from ten to twenty-four inches when grown. In the United States only two kinds noticeably exceed this two-foot limit; both of these are glass snakes (legless lizards) and they have excessively long tails. Next to these comes the Gila monster, with a maximum length of twenty-one and three-fourths inches, a maximum weight of four pounds twelve ounces. The chunky chuckwalla is the only one of our lizards that approaches the Gila monster in weight. The greatest length of the former falls three or four inches short of that of the latter, and this accounts chiefly for the difference in bulk.

Growth

REPTILES kept as pets, or even those in zoos, often grow very slowly and may wind up as dwarfs. This, the result of improper care, has brought about a belief that normal growth is slow. Nothing could be further from the truth. Somehow the giant tortoises have become symbols of this belief in slow growth; visitors to zoos like to stand in front of one and speculate on how much history has gone by since it was young. These visitors would be startled to know that a tortoise weighing three hundred and fifty pounds *may* be no more than twelve years old. This indicates a growth rate far greater than that of human beings. There is plenty of evidence that turtles in general grow about as fast as do the giant tortoises.

The most important landmark in the life of any animal is the age at which it first becomes able to reproduce. After reading that turtles grow at a good rate, it is not surprising to learn that they mature early. The hawksbill, one of the sea turtles, reproduces at the age of three

LIFE OF THE COLLARED LIZARD

KEYED TO PICTURES ON NEXT TWO PAGES

[A] IN LATE *August a male hatches from one of eight eggs buried five inches below the surface. He knows neither parent. He has a handsome black collar and bands across his back. He measures an inch and a half from tip of snout to base of tail. He is active for only seven weeks before going into a deep crevice for the winter.*

[B] LATE *the next spring, weeks after awakening from the six months of winter sleep, the collared lizard is almost four inches in length. He has lost his baby crossbands, and is ready to mate for the first time.*

[C] HIS *second spring finds him nearly grown to his full length, which will be a good four and a quarter inches excluding his tail.*

He is boss of an area from which he drives other males. He watches from the top of a rock and easily defeats intruders, sometimes in a short fight.

[D] ONE *of his mates is a female also in her second full summer. She is smaller and will never be his match in size and strength, nor will she have such bright colors. A few days after they mate, scarlet spots will appear along her sides, and remain for many weeks. Her eggs will be laid in late June, seventeen days after the mating. The eggs will hatch nine weeks later.*

The female first laid the previous summer when about a year old and this will be her second clutch. In some future years with very long warm seasons she will lay two clutches.

[E] COLLARED LIZARDS *live in the western United States and northern Mexico.*

[F] THEY *like dry, open, rocky country. There they find rocks for lookout posts, and plenty of sunshine. They prefer warm air (73°–91° F.) and enough sunshine to keep their bodies even warmer (100°–102° F.) than ours.*

Common chiggers live on collared lizards, but apparently do not harm them as they do man. The lizards shed their skin frequently, which keeps the number of chiggers from getting too great. During the warm months this shedding takes place about once every twenty-five days.

[G] BIRDS, *such as the road runner, and snakes devour many collared lizards. The victims are, for the most part, young lizards searching for new homes, and females heavy with eggs or busily digging nests. Watchfulness and agility enable many to escape.*

[H] THEY *eat many kinds of small creatures that are abroad during the day, but grasshoppers please them most of all. They catch their prey by rushing at it and seizing it in their jaws. They sometimes jump to catch animals flying above them.*

Collared lizards in a wild state apparently do not drink, although in captivity they will lap up drops or take water from a very shallow dish.

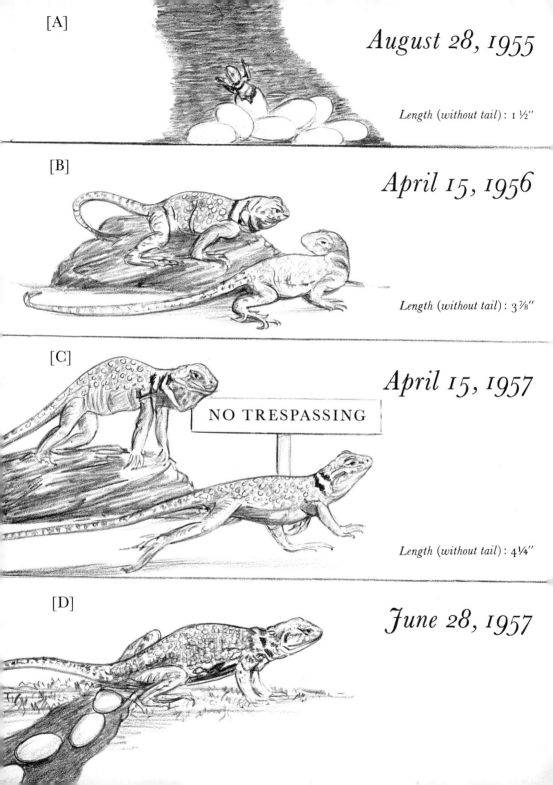

[A]

August 28, 1955

Length (without tail): 1 ½″

[B]

April 15, 1956

Length (without tail): 3 ⅞″

[C]

NO TRESPASSING

April 15, 1957

Length (without tail): 4¼″

[D]

June 28, 1957

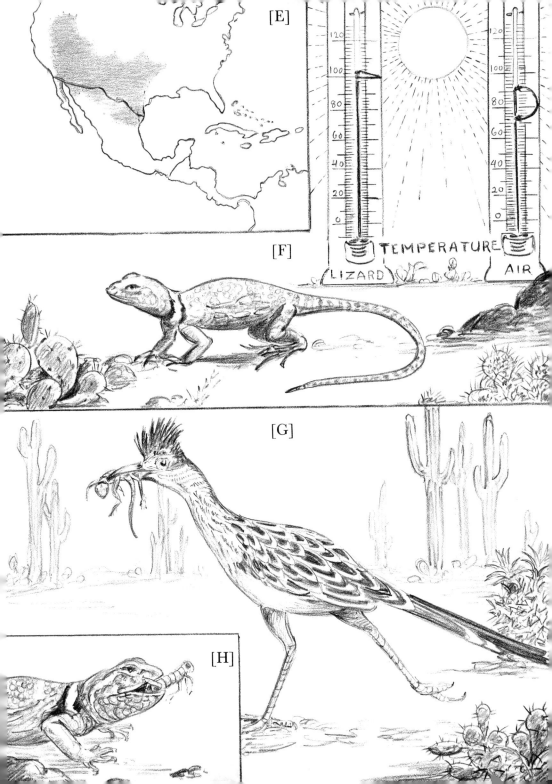

[E]

[F]

TEMPERATURE

LIZARD   AIR

[G]

[H]

years, and our own little box turtle at about four or five years of age. Its full growth is attained in much the same time as that of man himself: about twenty years.

Next to turtle growth rate, that of the crocodilians is most interesting. Although little or nothing is known about growth in most crocodilians, there is good information on the American alligator, which is probably typical. The facts that follow inform us about marked alligators living in a wild state, not just those kept in zoos. This marking of individuals living under natural conditions is a method now being widely used in scientific studies and the results have been highly worthwhile.

The average length of the alligator at two years of age is forty-one inches; at four years, sixty-two; at six, just six feet. During the sixth year the males begin to outstrip the females and reach a length of nine feet two inches when ten years old; at this time the females are two feet shorter and much lighter. The males, like giant tortoises, grow more rapidly than we do, reaching a weight of two hundred and fifty pounds at the age of ten. The females, on the other hand, when ten years old, weigh about as much as a small man (one hundred and twelve pounds).

The Indian python, Sylvia, that I kept as a pet grew fast enough in a few years to become an inconveniently long member of the family. Just how fast these giant snakes grow in the wilds has not been found out, though there is considerable information on the growth rate of small snakes.

For example, our common garter snake is, on the average, slightly less than seven inches long (head and body) at birth, seventeen or eighteen inches long when first ready to breed, and reaches a maximum length of about twenty-five inches. The females are able to mate when two years old, the males a little earlier. In Michigan, where this information was gathered by careful field studies, growth takes place only throughout the five warm months; the size of the snakes hardly changes during hibernation and immediately after. The infants increase about 18 per cent of their body length per month, but this rate decreases rapidly, especially after maturity. By the time a snake reaches the length of twenty inches, it adds only 1 or 2 per cent per month to its head-body length. We might add that the head-body length is used here because many garter snakes lose the tips of their tails and such losses make the use of total length impractical.

Perhaps the growth of lizards has been studied less than has that of either snakes or turtles. This is unfortunate because what we do know indicates that lizards reach extremes that may leave the growth rates of other reptiles far behind. Consider the true chameleons, those weird creatures found chiefly in Africa and Madagascar. These lizards apparently live less than three years, and yet the largest species reach a length of about two feet. Such big ones presumably have a lot of growing to do in a short time. The evidence of the chameleon's rapid growth is inferred, but we have substantial proof that a certain Asiatic and Pacific island gecko grows at an astounding rate and reaches sexual maturity about forty days after hatching. Even the American chameleon, namesake of the Old World chameleons just discussed, may

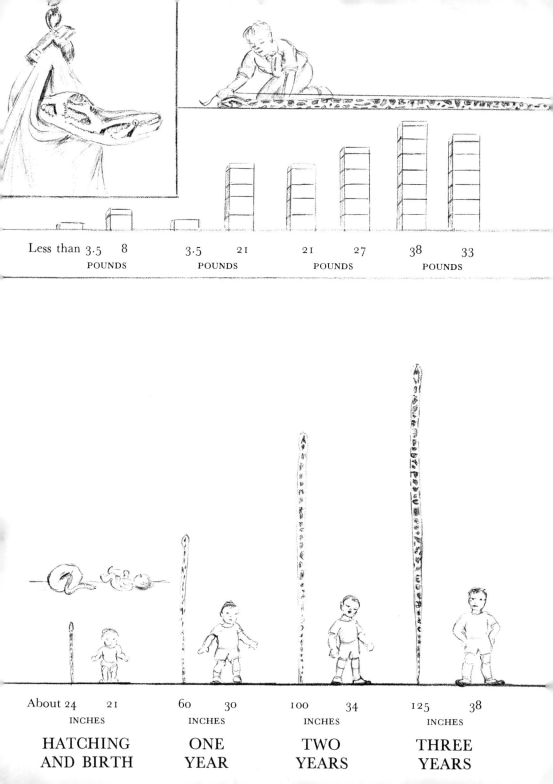

Less than 3.5   8
POUNDS

3.5   21
POUNDS

21   27
POUNDS

38   33
POUNDS

About 24   21
INCHES

60   30
INCHES

100   34
INCHES

125   38
INCHES

**HATCHING
AND BIRTH**

**ONE
YEAR**

**TWO
YEARS**

**THREE
YEARS**

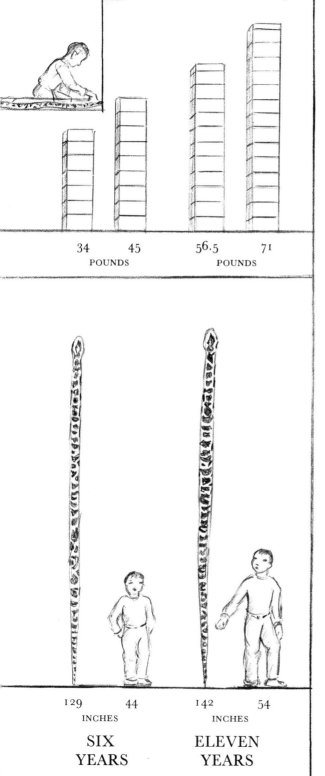

34 45   56.5   71
POUNDS   POUNDS

129   44   142   54
INCHES   INCHES

SIX   ELEVEN
YEARS   YEARS

JUDGING by Sylvia, an Indian python and a boy start life at much the same length. The python increases its length very fast and at a uniform rate until almost three years old. Then suddenly the rate of growth slows down to a snail's pace, and continues in this way for a long time, perhaps for the rest of life. The boy grows for less than a third of his life. His rate of growth is uneven and roughly equal to that of the python after it is three years old.

At birth, a boy is many times as heavy as a python. By the time both are three years old, the python has overtaken and passed the boy in weight. The python's rate of weight-increase then falls off, but the boy increases in weight at the same or an even greater rate for about eighteen more years. Sylvia's decrease in weight, from the end of her third year through her sixth year, obviously was not normal, and it is therefore impossible to do more than generalize about her later growth.

During her most rapid increase in length and weight, from one to nearly three years of age, Sylvia shed nine times and added thirty-four and one half pounds to her weight. She ate sixty-one pounds of food (one hundred and twenty-three rats). In short, she had to consume almost two pounds of rats to add one pound to her weight.

be ready to breed when less than a year old. There is evidence that the American chameleon also lives only about three years. This species is the Carolina anole of herpetologists. Just how fast the few giant species of anoles grow is not known, but a rapid growth may also be presumed for them. The Cuban anole, largest of all, reaches a total length of eighteen inches.

Future studies may show that many other lizards do not grow nearly as rapidly as do these chameleons and geckos. It is, however, a safe bet that great numbers of lizards need no more than three years to become sexually mature. Here is a rewarding field for the ambitious student of animal growth.

Age

"**H**OW long does a reptile live?"
This is a question that is easier to ask than to answer and one that needs amplifying. After we have determined which species of reptile the questioner has in mind, we shall find that there are two possible answers. One of these will answer the specific question, "How long does the average wild individual of a particular species live?" and the other, "How long will an individual of the same species be able to survive when it is protected from the ordinary dangers encountered by the reptile in the wild state?" Most wild animals, of course, are likely to meet with a violent end. If they are not killed by an enemy or a competitor, their death may be brought about by disease, starvation, or other "natural" means. (This sad situation is not too different from our own, is it? You may have read that "life expectancy" in the United States is now seventy years of age; that it was only thirty-four years of age, just seventy years ago; and that it is greater today, in this country, than it is in

many other parts of the world. This life expectancy figure is noticeably lower than the ninety, or more, years of age often reached by hardy persons.)

I'm not going to discuss the life expectancy of reptiles, as extremely little is known about it. What we do know, however, thanks to fine studies, is the greatest age attained by individual captive reptiles, mainly those in zoos. You will see that marked differences exist among the different groups of reptiles.

Turtles take first honors, although they are not the Methuselahs popular belief would make them. I have already pointed out that size is no factor because growth is rapid, and I add here that small species seem to live about as long as do giant ones. Our box turtle is now credited with an age as great as one hundred and thirty years, and there is evidence that one giant tortoise reached an age of one hundred and fifty-two. In the study mentioned above, five kinds of turtles were listed as having lived a hundred years or more. The age of turtles is not hard to study because it is so easy to mark their shells. This does not mean that every date found on a shell is valid; jokers are too fond of playing tricks by carving "G. Washington, 1751" or something else quite as ridiculous.

A large alligator farm in the southeastern part of this country likes to impress its many visitors by labeling pens with the supposed ages of the alligators in them. One sign may read "Three to four hundred years," another "Five hundred and over." Since there is no way to determine the age of old individuals, such information is fanciful guessing. The grain of truth here is that croc-

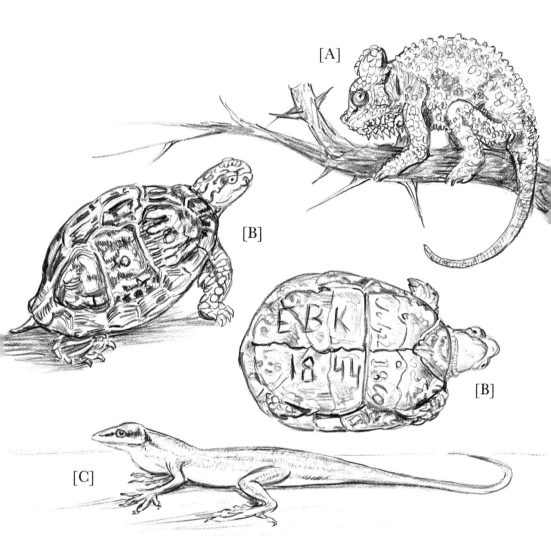

There is good evidence that this eastern box turtle [B] *survived a hundred and thirty years. It was discovered in 1953 near Hope Valley, Rhode Island, by Billy Johnson, who was born more than a century after this turtle was first marked.*

True chameleon [A] *and the American chameleon* [D], *at the other extreme, seem to live but a few years.*

odilians do live longer than any other reptiles except turtles. At least, the best evidence we have, that special study twice mentioned before, indicates as much. Among fifty-five kinds of reptiles known to have survived twenty years or more, there were thirty-one turtles, eleven crocodilians, ten snakes, and only two lizards. Three crocodilians had lived more than thirty years: a marsh crocodile, thirty-one years; a Chinese alligator, fifty years; and an American alligator, fifty-six years. No snake had survived more than twenty-eight years. In all fairness, we must add that an American alligator *may* have lived for eighty-five years in the *Jardin des Plantes*, the famous zoo of Paris, though some authorities dispute the validity of this record.

Two studies of snakes in captivity have been made: the one already referred to as listing ten kinds that lived twenty or more years, and another, more recent (1955) which was based only on snakes actually kept in this country. This second one records seven kinds for the twenty-and-more-years category. Since only two are duplicated, we have fifteen that have made the two-decades mark. These fifteen are scattered through snake classification and include large as well as small kinds. The record of twenty-eight years is held by an anaconda and a black-lipped cobra; a rainbow boa just missed it by living one year less. It is safe to consider that the potential life span of snakes is from twenty to thirty years. Apparently the turtles outlive man, the crocodilians fall well behind him, and the snakes come far behind these. It is interesting to recall at this point an important fact: Man outlives all other mammals.

In our main paragraph on lizard growth we stated that American as well as true chameleons apparently live little or no longer than three years. As far as we can tell, then, these are the most short-lived reptiles. At the other extreme, the information on lizards is not conclusive. That first careful world-wide study of reptile longevity gave only two lizards credit for reaching the twenty-year point. One of these, the so-called "slow-worm" of Europe, surpassed the snake record by surviving thirty-two years; the second barely made the list with only twenty. Two European glass snakes, also legless lizards, recently lived twenty-four and twenty-five years in the San Diego Zoo.

Many readers will wonder why we have not written of the time-honored counting of the "rattles" of rattlesnakes, and others may recall that turtle shells have growth rings indicating age. The segments of a rattler's rattle (the whole thing is the rattle, each separate part of it a segment) are useful only in young snakes because those on the end are constantly being lost through wear. Moreover, a segment is added, not once a year, but at each shedding, and a snake may shed three or four times a year. It all adds up to the fact that the segment count generally tells you about as much as you can determine from the size of the snake; after a good length is reached, neither size nor number of segments is of much use.

Turtle growth-ring counts are somewhat better than rattle-segment numbers. The chief trouble here is that the rings (ridges) are distinct only in young turtles growing rapidly, and become more and more difficult to count after maturity. In turtles living where growth is not regularly interrupted (by hibernation, for example), distinct ridges do not appear, and some kinds of turtles shed the outer layers in a way that makes the shell quite smooth.

Where Reptiles Live

BIRDS and mammals are much more widely spread out over the earth than are reptiles. This is because reptiles, being cold-blooded, cannot endure low temperatures, and, with the possible exception of sea turtles, reptiles are unable to migrate the way many birds and some mammals do. Wherever the ground becomes so deeply frozen in the wintertime that summer's thaw affects only the surface, you will find no reptiles, for reptiles cannot live there through the cold months. In moderately cold regions, reptiles hibernate. (See the chapter on various habits, which starts on page 72.)

Besides the reptiles, the only other backboned animals restricted by cold are the amphibians (frogs, salamanders, and their relatives). Their total distribution is much less than that of reptiles because amphibians have never taken to the seas. Fishes are cold-blooded as well as widely distributed; water does not change temperature as suddenly or as much as air. Furthermore, fishes are relatively resistant to low temperatures.

So much for broad generalizations. Coming now to geography, we can state that reptiles are found from tip to tip of South America, Africa, and Australia. On our continent they range to 60° N. latitude (central Canada). In Scandinavia alone do they reach the Arctic Circle and there they barely cross it. (The same ocean current that warms the British Isles enables snakes to range so far north in Scandinavia.) Thence eastward the reptile line crosses Europe and all of Asia, keeping parallel to, but well south of, the Arctic Circle. Many, but not all, of the remote islands of the great oceans are inhabited by limited numbers. All the continents except Australia have some mountains with tops too high and cold for reptiles.

It is not surprising that the crocodilians, with so few species living today, have the most limited distribution of all reptile groups. With the exception of the American and Chinese alligators, the crocodilians are animals of tropical regions. They are further limited to low altitudes and land areas. The salt-water crocodile, a giant of the Asiatic, Australian, and East Indian regions, is exceptional; it freely enters salt water to swim along coasts or from one island to another nearby. As explained in the chapter on ancient reptiles, crocodilians have not always been thus land-bound. Crocodilians are perhaps most numerous in Central and South America, where eight species live. Next comes Asia with six, and after that Africa (including Madagascar) with four, and Australia with but two.

The Chinese and American alligators now live far apart, but the fossil records show that their close relatives were once distributed around the world. The Chinese alligator is hard pressed by man, and appears to be near extinction. The American cousin has also been so badly persecuted that it now thrives only in the wilder parts of its original home. Early travelers described it as existing in vast numbers; it has even been stated that rivers could be crossed by using 'gators as steppingstones.

The turtles may be divided into two lots: a few marine kinds, and a large assortment of nonmarine species. The former are really at home in the tropical seas, although warm currents often carry them well beyond the tropics, and individuals may stray into cool waters as far as fifty degrees from the Equator. The vast majority of the breeding sites are within the tropics, and few eggs are laid north of the Tropic of Cancer or south of the Tropic of Capricorn.

The nonmarine turtles abound on all the continents except Europe, where only a few species live. All parts of Africa and Australia, except perhaps the extreme deserts, have their nonmarine turtles, whereas the southern end of South America and the colder parts of the northern continents are devoid of them. The greatest number of species is found in the eastern United States, central and southern Africa, and southeastern Asia.

Certain islands near Africa and also the Galápagos Islands, which lie on the Equator off the western coast of South America, have harbored hordes of giant tortoises during the time of recorded history. The early whale hunters all but exterminated these unique animals, which were an invaluable source of fresh meat.

From the point of view of total distribution, the snakes,

WHERE REPTILES LIVE

NUMBER OF SYMBOLS INDICATES RELATIVE ABUNDANCE OF SPECIES

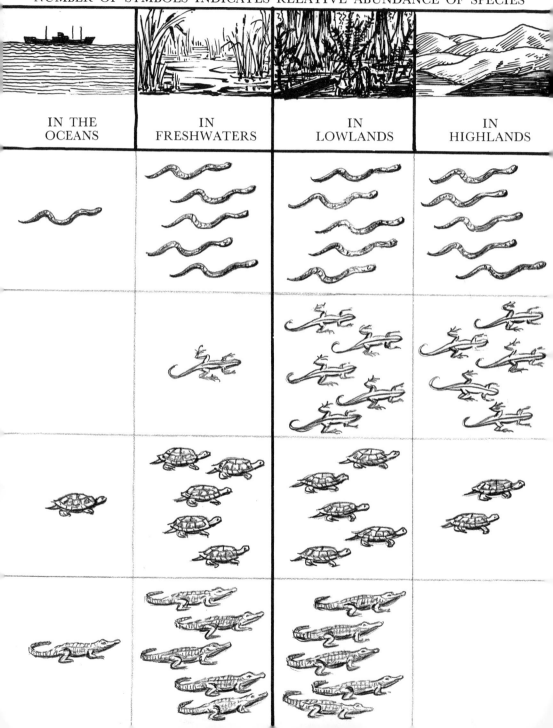

| IN THE OCEANS | IN FRESHWATERS | IN LOWLANDS | IN HIGHLANDS |

WHERE REPTILES LIVE

NUMBER OF SYMBOLS INDICATES RELATIVE ABUNDANCE OF SPECIES

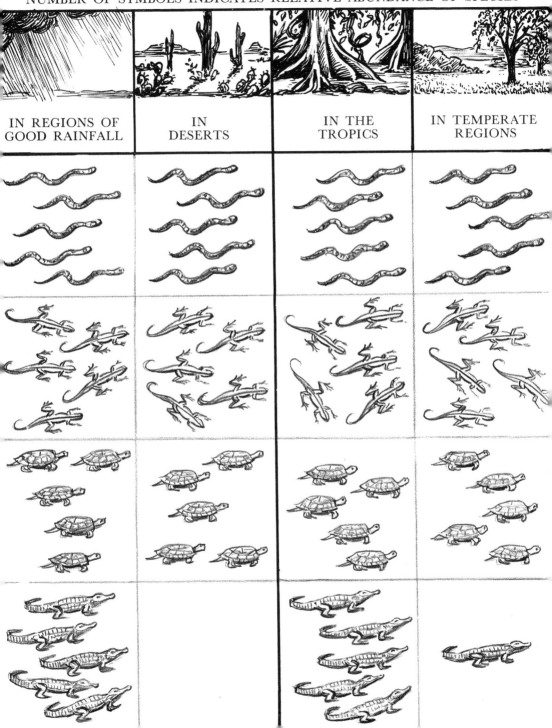

| IN REGIONS OF GOOD RAINFALL | IN DESERTS | IN THE TROPICS | IN TEMPERATE REGIONS |

like the turtles, must be divided into two very unequal lots, the few sea snakes and the innumerable nonmarine species. These sea snakes, in sharp contrast to the marine turtles, are by no means world-wide in range. Only one among some fifty known species has strayed far from the headquarters of the group, the region lying between southeastern Asia and northern Australia. This fellow, the yellow-bellied sea snake, has crossed the Indian Ocean to African coasts, the Pacific Ocean to American shores. The Atlantic Ocean is devoid of snakes. The sea snakes have nothing to do with the mythical and gigantic sea serpents. Sea snakes are not even unusually large snakes, the average length being three or four feet, the maximum nine and a fraction.

The hordes of nonmarine snakes are distributed around the world with a great concentration of species living in the tropics. Among reptiles, only the lizards approach them in number of species. In total distribution on the continents, the lizards and snakes are alike, except in North America; both of them range to the extremities of the southern continents and barely cross the Arctic Circle in Scandinavia, but fall well short of it in Eurasia east of Scandinavia. In North America the snakes are the only reptiles that get very far across the Canadian border, a garter snake ranging as far as extreme southern Northwest Territories (60° N.) or some six and a half degrees south of the Arctic Circle. The lizards go about as far as 51° N. (British Columbia).

Lizards are certainly the most land-minded of reptiles. Although in ages past they have taken to the oceans, there is no sea-going lizard alive today. The nearest approach to this is the giant "marine" iguana of the Galápagos Islands, which feeds on sea plants but lives almost entirely on land. There are relatively few lizards that can be called aquatic; all the crocodilians, great numbers of turtles, and many snakes are, at least to some degree, water-going. As if to carry the matter to a still greater extreme, the lizards are the most successful of reptiles to be found living under semidesert to desert conditions. Two further points are of considerable interest. In spite of their inability to cope with the seas, lizards are the most abundant nonmarine reptiles on small, remote oceanic islands, and they are the reptiles that man most frequently carries by accident across the oceans. No fewer than seven kinds of lizards have been added to the fauna of the United States in this way.

Some facts about lizard distribution have been given above in the discussion of snakes.

Enemies and Defense

FROM the point of view of self-defense, the four groups of reptiles fall into two lots: the crocodilians and turtles in one, the snakes and lizards in the other. The reptiles of the first lot are protected by a tough outer covering or armor; those of the second, with few exceptions, lack such a covering. The exceptions are certain lizards that have bony plates in the skin, but even these are hardly in a class with turtles and crocodilians.

Not only is the skin of the crocodilian tough, but it is also reinforced on the animal's back with little plates of bone. Some have these plates imbedded in the skin of the belly also. Other impressive characteristics of the crocodilian are its great size and its powerful jaws set with long teeth. Small wonder that the fully grown crocodilian has relatively few enemies! Among reptiles, the crocodilian stands alone in making tail and jaws work together in defense. If an animal is foolish enough to get near the crocodilian's body, a swift sideswipe of its massive tail will knock the victim toward the jaws, which have been quickly opened and placed where the victim will land. The jaws of a crocodilian that is more than ten feet long are powerful enough to crush the larger bones of a cow.

In the life cycle of even the armored reptiles there is a period of weakness. This begins when the egg is laid, and extends through the first months after hatching. The egg is a delicacy to many kinds of animals, especially mammals. Hatchlings, too, are frequently devoured by them. The crocodilian female that guards her nest until the hatchlings have escaped, shows superiority to the turtle. Turtle eggs and hatchlings are left to the fickle care of fate. Though the turtle shell develops rapidly enough, at the time of hatching it gives little protection. Many tiny turtles in part make up for this weakness by an astonishing ability to hide. It is the hatchling sea turtle that faces the great trial of having to cross a sandy beach to reach the safety of the sea. Even when the water is reached, hungry fish may lurk at its edge and swallow the baby turtle before it can conceal itself.

Few of the backboned animals are as well protected as the turtle. In its extreme development, the turtle's shell is so complete that, when closed, a thin knife blade cannot be forced into any of the cracks between the upper and lower parts. The shell of our box turtles is a fine example; the hinge across the lower shell or plastron allows it to close neatly against the carapace. You almost wonder how a frightened box turtle manages to breathe. The shell is usually made up of an outer layer of horny stuff similar to our fingernails and an inner one of bone, which includes the ribs and backbone. There is a lot of variation, but the vast majority of shells give excellent protection. The fact that turtles have used a shell for some two hundred million years is certainly good evidence of its value.

Before passing to snakes and lizards, that second and relatively unprotected lot, I should like to make a few remarks about the so-called "struggle for existence" in nature. This, more vividly named the "rule of tooth and claw," implies to most of us that the lives of animals and plants are one continuous battle, with the physically strong coming out on top. Some of the early champions of the theory of evolution took great joy in describing that side of life. Many scientific studies show that two things are wrong with this idea. In the first place, animals and plants must work together harmoniously as much as they must struggle. We are being just as truthful and much more pleasant when we change those phrases to the "co-operation for existence" or the "rule of 'give a hand.' " The evolution of life from the simple to the complex has called for an incredible amount of love and teamwork. You may place the emphasis where you please. In the second place, we are learning more and more that even the "struggle" is often anything but a fight. Many animals use more subtle means of coming out on top. These we call bluffing (by an animal that cannot put up a good fight); warning (by an animal that can, but prefers not to fight); and simple flight. The Chinese long ago made the saying, "There are thirty-six ways of escaping, but the best of all is just to run away." Even in warfare among human beings, this way has been used to great advantage.

Because many snakes are venomous and most of them bite, they are commonly thought to be great fighters. The more we learn about them the more it becomes clear that they are better at warning, bluffing, and fleeing than they are at fighting. Many of the dangerous snakes, when annoyed give ample notice before biting, and still others are averse to using their fangs. At first thought it might seem foolish for deadly creatures to bother to warn; further thought may bring to mind the fact that, in avoiding a close conflict, these animals save their venom, which they need in getting food, and often avoid physical injury. What is the advantage to the snake if it kills the enemy but loses its own life? The snake wisely prefers to protect itself, if possible, and live as long as it can.

The rattlesnakes and the cobras are the best-known warners. Oddly enough, among venomous species, only the rattlers have a warning method not used by harmless snakes, and even the forerunner of the rattle can be seen in the vibrating tail of many other snakes. The famous hood of the cobra is only an extreme development of a neck-and-head-flattening habit found in various groups. It is often thought that the cobras are copied or mimicked by harmless snakes that in this way pass themselves off as venomous. More likely the habit developed first in the harmless snakes, since these gave rise to the venomous ones. This whole subject of mimicry in nature is a fascinating one, but it is too lengthy for us to consider here.

You might think that an animal with such a simple shape as a snake would have a hard time developing many different ways of warning or bluffing. If so, the following brief account of some of these ways may prove surprising. Do not forget that three have already been mentioned: rattling, vibrating the tail (in dry vegetation this makes a noise), and flattening the head and neck. Hissing is one of the commonest methods and often goes with expanding the body by filling the lungs with air. In a few snakes the hiss is noticeably amplified by the

REPTILE TAILS (*see opposite page*) *are often useful in dealing with dangers. The rattlesnake's rattle is made up of many segments linked together loosely but securely. In a young snake, the rattle* [A] *is pointed; in an old one, the rattle* [B] *is about as wide at the tip as at the base. This old rattle has been* x-*rayed to show the bony core that supports it. Several end bones of the spine have grown together to form this core.*

A skunk [C] *is puzzled by the breaking of a lizard's tail, which will be replaced. A lizard* [D] *may even get a forked tail as the result of the original one being partly severed.*

The American crocodile [E] *uses the tail as well as the jaws in defense.*

The automobile (see below) brings death to many snakes.

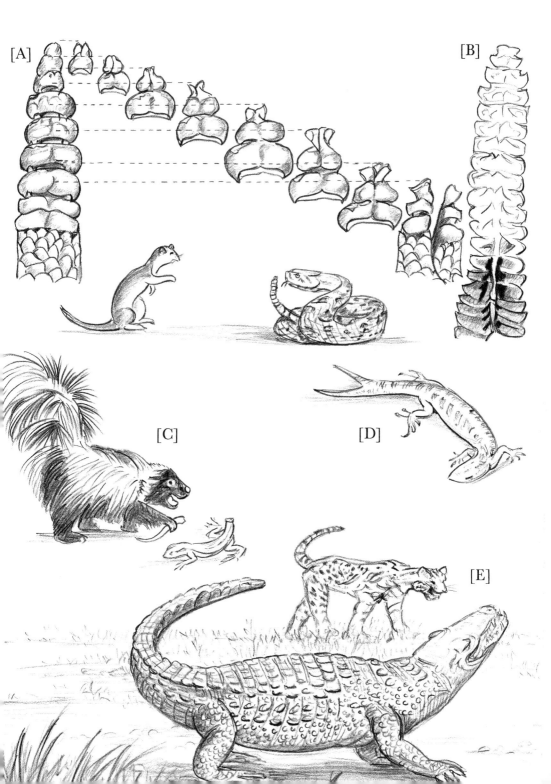

[A]

[B]

[C]

[D]

[E]

vibration of a vertical flap just in front of the windpipe. Many snakes raise the head and neck off the ground, and a few even make the tail look like a head by raising and moving it while keeping the head down. Causing bright colors to appear suddenly is another trick and it is closely linked with elevating some part of head or body, flattening, or blowing. Finally, I shall briefly mention other tricks: striking without actually biting, making a bad odor, rolling up into a tight ball, freezing ("playing 'possum"), and weaving the body.

In some respects lizards and snakes are very similar in their methods of dealing with their enemies. Both are great bluffers as well as masters at the art of concealment, and the methods used to inspire fear may be similar: puffing up, hissing, or assuming an alarming pose, and so on. The lizards either lack or make little use of certain snake specialties, but have gone much further in other directions, or even developed new lines of their own. It is an odd fact, already pointed out, that only two species of lizards, our own Gila monster and its near relative, the Mexican beaded lizard, are venomous. Contrast this with the hundreds of kinds of venomous snakes so generously spread around the world.

If the lizards have not made the most of their head ends, they have gone to great extremes with their tails. The snakes, as we have just seen, were satisfied to vibrate the tail or even make it behave like a head, but the lizards have found unusual uses for tails. The greatest of these is tail-dropping to confound an enemy. This might seem like a drastic way to escape, but, to the lizard with a tail made to come apart, so to speak, its loss causes

only slight injury. The skin is torn but a vertebra comes
in two at a weak point near or at its middle, and the
muscles separate neatly, leaving, on the stump, several
cone-shaped depressions that bleed very little. A new
but inferior tail soon appears. A partial break will sometimes cause a second tail to grow out even though the
first was not lost. The tail, in some lizards, is so fragile
that you cannot take hold of it even gently without having it come off in your hand. That, of course, is just
what the lizard wants. While you are figuring out what
happened, the owner gets away. To make matters better
for the lizard and worse for you or any hungry animal,
the tail wiggles about. This attracts your attention and
perhaps keeps the hungry animal from realizing that it
has been fooled; after all, part of a tail is better than
nothing.

All lizards do not have fragile tails, though a great
many do, and, in some, the tail just about wags the body.
Our own glass snakes (three species) are an example of
this. These snakelike lizards have no limbs and a tail
more than twice as long as head and body. It is clear that
one of these reptiles will come apart at a point much
nearer to its snout than to the tip of the tail. Man himself is as badly fooled as any other animal; he makes up
the most fantastic tales about the way glass snakes behave. One can, it is commonly said, break up and then,
when danger has passed, reassemble and proceed on its
way none the worse for wear. Of course no glass snake
can join itself together even if broken in only two parts,
nor can the body itself be severed into parts. That they
do often use the tail-dropping trick is shown by the fact

that from one-half to three-fourths of the glass snakes found in a wild state have new tails. Just how often an individual can pull this trick has never been found out. The second tail is never as good as the first, so there are limits.

What animals, then, manage to get around all these many ways reptiles have of defending themselves? It goes without saying that man is the archenemy. This is due to several things: his groundless fear of lizards and harmless snakes, his appetite for turtle soup, and the value he places on the innumerable objects made of reptile leather. Next to man come numerous other mammals, among them opossums, armadillos, skunks, badgers, raccoons, cats, dogs, rats, hogs, deer, and mongooses. Although plenty of snakes, both venomous and harmless, are eaten by mongooses, the snake-eating habits of these agile mammals have been grossly overrated. Some mongooses do not eat any snakes, and most of them probably live largely on other creatures. It has been said that Kipling's famous story about Rikki-tikki-tavi is to blame for the exaggerated belief that Asiatic mongooses are destroyers of dangerous snakes, but Kipling probably based his story on widespread Asiatic folklore.

Birds also number among the enemies of reptiles. As destroyers of snakes, secretary birds are believed to stand among birds as the mongooses do among mammals, but these long-legged birds have no monopoly. (Incidentally, this interesting long-legged African bird was given its name because of its erectile crest that resembles a bunch of quill pens ·stuck behind the ear.) Serpent eagles eat countless numbers of reptiles, as do many other birds of prey. Even chickens and turkeys take their toll of small snakes and lizards.

Strangest of all is the fact that snakes are one of their own worst enemies, though this does not make them natural cannibals. A snake that eats another species of snake may be no more a cannibal than a man who eats a monkey. It just happens that one snake is perfectly shaped to be swallowed by another, and the other does not have to be smaller. Many people go so far as to say that our king snakes are sworn enemies of rattlers, but this belief is not really true. King snakes do eat other snakes, but these snake-eaters show no preference for venomous ones, and their diet includes various other animals. Many other snakes show a much greater fondness for a snake diet than do the king snakes. Certain cobras and coral snakes, for example, appear to eat nothing but snakes and lizards (snake-eating snakes will also devour lizards). Snake-eaters are so common that we have the adjective ophiophagous to designate them.

Various Habits

WE have learned how reptiles eat, how they reproduce, and how they defend themselves. Let us turn now to how the reptile makes use of space. Is he an aimless wanderer, or does he stake out a home area? If he does, how big is it, and can he get back to it if taken away? Studying reptile home areas calls for a lot of very careful work carried on for long stretches of time; it also calls for special little tricks such as using small tags that the reptile either does not mind or is not conscious of wearing.

The coming of winter forces a cold-blooded animal to do one of two things: get out or get under, to put it briefly. The reptile is a poor traveler to begin with, and has never developed the ability to get out. This means it must get under or into some protecting material. After all, it is simpler to go straight downward a few feet than to crawl hundreds of miles. We admire the bird for seeming to know that better conditions prevail hundreds of miles away, but what about the reptile's apparent knowledge that low temperatures do not penetrate more than a few feet into the ground? Did *you* know this? In places with heavy snowfall, the snow itself acts like a blanket, and penetration is still less.

Long migrations call for great strength as well as ability to travel fast and find the way through new and unmarked areas. Going into the ground, though simpler, has its price, too. The hibernating reptile must do without food. It obviously misses a lot of living, torpidity being the result of slowed breathing and heart action. Even development of embryos is suspended. In spite of existing without food, the torpid reptile must not be thought of as starving; careful measurements have shown that surprisingly little weight is lost. You will recall that the average well-fed reptile is ready to survive a year of starvation even though active all the while. What are a mere three to five months of winter sleep?

Several questions spring to mind at the thought of a hibernating animal. What type of site is chosen and how is it found? How does the reptile get below the surface? Is it alone? If not, is the company good or bad? Most of these are much easier to ask than to answer.

To begin with, the sites are so varied that they all but defy generalization. The most romantic are the widely publicized rattlesnake "dens," caves, or cavelike cavities usually in rugged hills or mountains, though almost any deep crevice or cavity will do. The reptile may even work its own way into very soft earth or debris. The colder the country, the deeper the penetration. During the winter, at one place in this country, low temperatures (even to minus 40°F.) did not send the earth's temperature quite to the freezing point four feet below the surface; a thick blanket of snow covered the ground. A reptile would certainly have survived at that depth or even a little nearer the surface. No one knows just how a den is started, but it is known that snakes often return to the same den, one following the trail made by another. This may lead you to conclude that reptiles always collect in great numbers to pass the winter. Such is not the case; at times only a few individuals reach the same site. Study has shown, however, that there is advantage in group hibernation. Moisture is required, and a lot of reptiles coiled together keep moisture in. It is interesting that a truce may be called; a species sometimes passes the winter in close company with another that it ordinarily eats with gusto.

In certain parts of the world dry seasons combined with high temperatures force reptiles into a period of greatly reduced activity something like hibernation. This state, known as estivation, helps cold-blooded animals, which are only a little better able to endure great heat than severe cold. The lack of built-in temperature controls, as well as insulating fur and feather, puts these creatures at the mercy of extreme changes in temperature. Reptiles, with their dry skins, do not have to estivate in as many places as do amphibians (frogs, salamanders, and relatives) and fishes, with their moist skins.

It is an odd fact that among all living reptiles only the few sea turtles seem to make any real use of space. These large reptiles swim hundreds of miles from feeding ground to breeding beach. Even though there can be little doubt about these long trips, no one has ever tagged numbers of individuals at a feeding ground and found them again on a breeding beach, or vice versa. Doing this would remove the last shreds of doubt.

With the sea turtles out of the way, it can be stated that reptiles move about very little. The reptilian point of view seems to be,"Here I came into the world and here I sit as long as I can find food, shelter, and a mate. This spot owes me a living." Some running about is of course necessary, but, as far as we know, reptiles rarely go more than a mile or two from the place of birth or hatching. The vast majority even live within an area an acre or so in extent; that is, one not larger than a city block. The biggest movements are to hibernation dens or to places with enough water. Movements to the latter are made by aquatic species living in areas where the water level changes with the seasons. There is not a great deal of difference among the groups of reptiles. Turtles, chiefly the aquatic ones, and crocodilians probably go farther, reaching the one- or two-mile limit. Snakes and lizards, especially snakes, are satisfied with much less movement, and often have ranges considerably less than a thousand feet (about a fifth of a mile) in diameter.

So far so good: a reptile is a stay-at-home. But how does a reptile feel about other individuals of the species and its home area; are they welcome or are they looked upon as intruders? The question cannot yet be answered fully, though some facts have been established. A fair number of male lizards adopt definite areas and defend them against all comers of the same species except submissive females. Further study will probably prove this to be a common lizard habit. Among other reptiles, only certain crocodilians are known to have comparable behavior.

Newspapers often print stories of amazing "homing" ability—stories that tell of animals finding their way back after they have been taken hundreds of miles away and turned loose. If there were any reptile capable of doing this, it would, indeed, be a turtle—but it would probably be a marine, rather than a land turtle. I have written of the long migrations almost certainly made by sea turtles; animals that make such journeys may be assumed to have homing ability. After the marine species, land and fresh-water turtles are the best homing reptiles. Some of these can return a distance of almost two miles; many others apparently cannot do as well.

One especially interesting habit of snakes at first confused and now puzzles students of reptiles: the so-called combat "dance" of males. This looks like courtship, and has been described as such even by trained observers who failed to examine the dancers to check their sex. Herpetologists have not finally determined the meaning of the dance. Perhaps it is a poorly developed contest over territory, or it may be a social struggle, one male trying to test his strength against another. It does seem to have sexual implications, but just what these are nobody knows.

The remarkable thing about these combats is that neither tooth nor fang is brought into play; one male tries to wear the other out physically rather than seriously injure him. The "dancing" of large male snakes is very impressive. Here is a brief description of the "dance" of one highly venomous species that often grows to be

An intruding male black iguana is being challenged by the ruling male of a section of rock wall in Mexico. A female watches from below. To threaten, a male nods the head, holds the mouth open, distends the throat, and flattens the sides. Rivals seldom have actual fights because the intruder usually retreats. Black iguanas often have a total length of three feet.

Australian brown snakes as well as Australian black snakes indulge in violent combat "dances." The two males shown here are brown snakes.

six feet long. With arched necks and raised heads two Australian black snakes spar for advantage, each trying to get his head above the other's. When one succeeds, he violently wraps his body about that of his opponent until the two look like strands of a single rope. Furiously writhing and hissing, the snakes squeeze each other as they roll over and over. After about a minute of struggle and as if by signal, the round ends and both males get ready for another. The decision comes when one is too tired to go on. Wrestling pairs may even be picked up without separating. Combat dancing has been seen on four continents, and, therefore, must be a widespread habit of snakes.

Reptile Relationships

HAVING written several chapters on reptiles themselves, I shall now tell how reptiles originated and what animals evolved from them. In the chapter that follows we shall turn to reptiles of ancient times.

It must be kept in mind that we are dealing entirely with backboned animals (vertebrates), and any generalizations made apply to them and to them only. As we read in the first chapter, backboned animals are few in number when compared with the vast array of those without backbones (invertebrates), but to us (members of the vertebrate group ourselves) the vertebrates are much more important than their proportionate numbers would indicate. The invertebrates (insects, worms, spiders, mollusks, and so on) number many more than a million species, whereas the vertebrates (fishes, amphibians, reptiles, birds, and mammals) number no more than thirty-five thousand.

Some three to four hundred million years ago the fishes were the predominant vertebrate animals. That

time in the earth's history is known as the Silurian and
Devonian periods, and these rather pleasant names will
forever be chiefly associated with fishes. Indeed, those
ancient fishes had little competition; reptiles, birds, and
mammals did not yet exist. Life in water has its advantages. Locomotion is easy and the body does not dry up,
nor do the eggs; changes in temperature are not sudden,
and oxygen is readily taken from the water by gills.

Near the end of the Devonian period, some of the
fishes became, so to speak, dissatisfied with the easy life
in water, and took steps toward the land. This meant
that they had to get (1) something better than fins for
locomotion, (2) a body-covering, as well as eggs, that
would resist drying, and (3) a method of extracting
oxygen from the air instead of from the water. These
were big problems and there were many others. The
dissatisfied fishes somehow overcame all difficulties except
the egg-drying problem, and they managed to get
around that one by makeshift: they went back to the
water to lay eggs, which meant that the young had to
live for a time in water.

Perhaps you have already guessed the name of these
progressive deserters from the fish camp. They were the
first amphibians, and it is not hard to see why their name
comes from two Greek words, one meaning "double"
and another meaning "life." The amphibians developed
rapidly, and for a few tens of millions of years were the
ruling land animals. Some were large and others had odd
shapes. Today their remote descendants, spread around
the globe, are known as frogs (including toads), salamanders, and cæcilians. The frogs are doing very well,

rating not far behind the snakes and lizards, whereas the salamanders, much less successful, are about on a par with the turtles, though not nearly so broadly distributed. The cæcilians are burrowing, worm-shaped amphibians of the tropics; they are few in number and known only to students.

The rule of the amphibians was brief because they soon had to compete with a new lot of progressives which were introducing a brand-new idea for backboned animals: complete freedom from water. Leading that double life proved to have its drawbacks as the new line, the very earliest reptiles, was soon to show. The breaking of this final link called for the development of an entirely different and vastly more complex egg, an egg that would not easily dry up. If you have ever seen the jellylike egg masses of frogs or salamanders, you know how simple each egg is compared with that of a hen; reptile eggs are seen by few but they are basically like those we eat for breakfast. The chief difference is that the bird egg is much more thoroughly protected from drying. When you look at the developing egg of a frog, you are seeing the embryo itself, whereas the embryo of the reptile or bird egg is not only enclosed in the shell but surrounded by a strong protective sac called the amnion. Finding the embryo when it has just begun to develop calls for some effort. The next time you eat an egg, stop to consider that it is one of the chief keys to *your* existence, one of the reasons why you are a human being, living in a house, instead of an aquatic creature.

So much for the relatives of reptiles that came before them; what about those that followed, the birds and mammals? For tens of millions of years the reptiles did very well indeed, and no doubt the conservatives among them were satisfied. However, just as one group of fishes had headed for the land and developed into amphibians, and a group of these had shaken off that bondage of water and become the reptiles, so certain reptiles had a strong urge of their own, too. This was to develop that internal heating system mentioned in the last chapter. The interesting thing this time was that two unrelated groups of reptiles had the same urge, one developing into the birds, the other into the mammals. Internal heating is helped by good external covering, as every one of you knows from wearing clothes. The birds solved the problem with feathers, the mammals with fur. You are already wondering what happened to your fur, and in doing so you are raising a question to which science has no very good answer. You do know that human beings who live in cold places must use clothing to take the place of that lost fur.

To the people of cold regions, or of cities anywhere, reptiles seem to be a very unimportant and well-hidden part of animal life. But if we use our imagination, that part of the mind so dear to us, and think of life as a whole (that is, the development of life in our animal kingdom) the picture changes somewhat. For fully a third of the time that vertebrates have been significant, the reptiles have been predominant, and even today one species of vertebrate among every six is a reptile. Reptiles are still spread evenly throughout the warmer parts of the earth. Reptiles hold a central and key position. The fishes and amphibians came before them but the

The ancient reptile, Seymouria [A], surrounded by three of its primitive relatives: a fish, Osteolepis [B], an amphibian, Diplovertebron [C], a bird, Archaeopteryx [D], and a mammal, Prodiacodon [E].

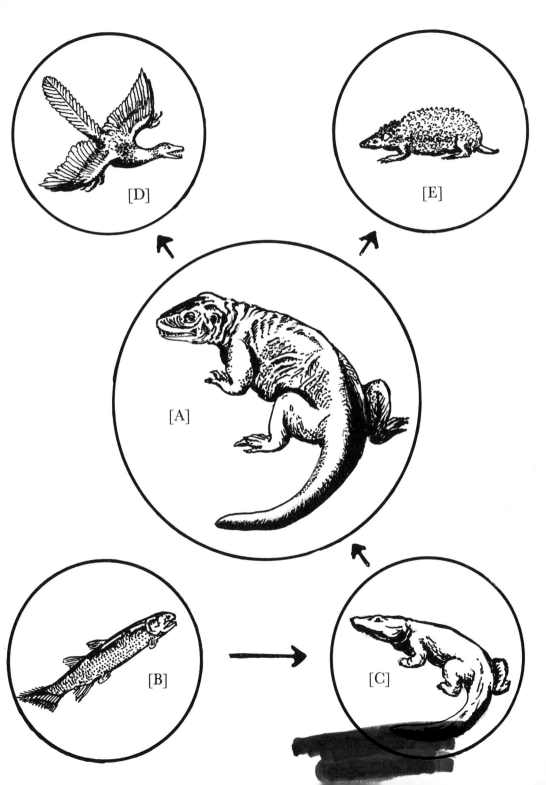

reptiles improved on these; as a result, the mammals and birds that followed were able to make further improvements. Doesn't all of this constitute sufficient claim to distinction? Finally, for reasons not entirely clear, reptiles, especially snakes, arouse deep and diverse emotions in us: both fear and reverence. It is certain, though, that we are not born with these, even the fear of snakes being acquired.

Reptiles of Ancient Times

ALTHOUGH this is a book about the reptiles of today, no doubt you are interested in how these living reptiles compare with those that roamed the earth in ages past. Three major facts must be emphasized at once: reptiles have been on the earth a long time; those alive today are a mere remnant; reptiles were once the ruling animals.

When I state that reptiles have been on this earth for a long time, I mean that they have been here long if measured in the periods of time that we human beings usually use: years, centuries, and millenniums (thousand-year-periods). Geologists deal with such long stretches of time that they do not like to think in terms of years, but they are kind enough to make rough estimates for the sake of nongeologists. In considering the periods of years about to be given, you must remember that they are by no means exact down to a few thousands of years. The first reptiles probably appeared two hundred and fifty million years ago. In comparison, man is generally granted a geological age of one million years, and the earth itself is two billion years old.

If you get a book on classification, you will see at once that the reptiles alive today (about fifty-five hundred species) are in truth a mere remnant. First sight of that book will make you want to close it quickly because of the hundreds of long names it gives. Granting that you overcome this and study the lists of names, not one by one, but from a broad point of view, you will learn some interesting facts. Students usually divide reptiles into sixteen big groups or orders. Among these sixteen, only four have living members. This alone suggests that the reptiles we see around us fall far short of being the whole show.

But let us consider one by one the four orders with living members. The first order (Chelonia) is made up of turtles, and has many names of groups no longer alive. Turtles, with their hard shells, leave the best fossils, and the record shows that the turtles have repeated the history of the reptiles themselves. The vast majority of them have long since departed from this earth.

Next you will read the saddest story of all, that of the order Rhynchocephalia, the "beakheads." These reptiles, formerly spread around the globe, are found today only on little islands of New Zealand where but a single kind lives. This lizardlike reptile, the tuatara, once on the verge of extinction, is at present protected by an enlightened government.

Third, you will come to the one reptilian order with a name that you recognize: Crocodilia. The living crocodilians, only twenty-three in number of species, are not

The harmless little tuatara lives today, whereas Tyrannosaurus rex, ancient lord of reptiles, must be sought in dinosaur exhibits.

to be compared with the great array of fossil crocodilians. Even the twenty-three are, of course, a much better representation than is the poor little tuatara of New Zealand, which I like to call the most lonesome of reptiles.

Last of the four and lowest on the list stands the flourishing order Squamata,"the scaled ones." These, the snakes and lizards, comprise about 95 per cent of all living reptiles. Snakes and lizards do not fossilize well because of their weak skeletons, and we shall never know how many may have died out without leaving signs in the rocks. It is probable, however, that they did not become predominant until comparatively recent times.

We know now that the relative importance of reptiles has varied at different times in their long history. We know that today they are by no means as dominant as are the mammals, and scarcely as conspicuous as the birds. If we turn the clock back a very few million years, we come to a time when man did not exist, but the mammals were still dominant. Another turn, this time one of about sixty million years, and we find the mammals far from dominant. This is the end of the Age of Reptiles, which itself lasted more than twice as long as that of mammals. During this great period of reptile life, all but two of those sixteen orders existed, and these two were unimportant groups of early transient types. The dinosaurs, which made up two whole orders, are popularly used as symbols of the Age of Reptiles, but, obviously, they were only a small if important part of the whole show. To put it mildly, reptiles were rampant during this era. The mammals came into existence during the first part of the Age of Reptiles; little is known about their early history and they were as insignificant during that age as the reptiles were dominant. The mammals blossomed in the following era, the Age of Mammals, as effectively as the reptiles had blossomed during the preceding era.

Space would not allow me to describe even a few of the reptiles that vanished so completely, but I shall show how they spread themselves over the earth, taking great advantage of the possibilities of land, sea, and air. In contrast, the reptiles of today make little use of the seas, and almost none of the air. Nearly half of those sixteen orders of reptiles included distinctly marine types, and two orders were made up entirely of such. These two were the fishlike ichthyosaurs and the long-necked, paddle-limbed plesiosaurs (and close relatives). There were aquatic dinosaurs, and even the lizards of those times had their marine kinds, the mosasaurs of almost world-wide distribution. It is not surprising that the early crocodilians refused to be outdone, and developed a group of fully marine species.

It is hardly necessary to emphasize the existence of great numbers of land reptiles in those times. The dinosaurs no doubt were the most conspicuous as well as the most varied, making up, you will recall, two whole orders. The maximum size and the grotesque shapes of these creatures are well known, but not everybody realizes that some kinds were small, no bigger than rabbits. It has already been pointed out that aquatic dinosaurs existed. As to the air, some of the most peculiar reptiles that ever lived made ample use of it: the pterosaurs. These had hollow bones like birds, and enormous wingspread. They were usually small, although one giant species measured as much as twenty-seven feet from wing tip to wing tip.

Also interesting is the fact that birds had their beginning in the Age of Reptiles, though they are not directly descended from the pterosaurs, as you might imagine. Birds, along with pterosaurs, crocodilians, and both orders of dinosaurs, did, however, stem from the same bipedal reptiles. The backboned animals first took to the air about the middle of the Age of Reptiles, and now, at long last, man himself has done so in imitation of reptiles, birds, and other mammals.

Dangerous Reptiles

IS it dangerous?'' This is the first question to be asked about most strange animals. With reptiles, however, the first question will most likely be, *"How* dangerous is it?'' The belief that all reptiles are dangerous is far from true. Considering the word "dangerous" as meaning either large and ferocious or effectively venomous, not more than one species in twenty or twenty-five is dangerous. No one can give an exact figure because opinions differ widely; many a ferocious reptile and venomous snake is too small to do appreciable harm; some large venomous snakes seldom bite.

In the United States and Canada, for instance, I rate the American crocodile (large and ferocious), the Gila monster (venomous lizard), and eighteen species of snakes (fifteen of them rattlesnakes) as dangerous. The total number of species of reptiles found in these two countries is two hundred and thirty-six, one hundred and fourteen of them snakes. In the whole northwestern quarter of the United States, the only dangerous reptile is the prairie rattlesnake.

Let us see how the major groups of reptiles compare in this respect, beginning with the most harmless. No turtle can be called dangerous, though this does not mean you should carelessly put your hand within reach of a large sea turtle or even one of our own snappers. If you do forget this advice, the injury you might sustain will be far from serious. I know of one sea turtle which, instead of biting, splashed water at anyone who refused to scratch its shell. That turtle was as friendly as a dog. Even our alligator snapping turtle, said to be able to bite a broomstick in two, can do no such thing. An actual test showed that one of these snappers weighing some forty pounds could scarcely break a pencil. This snapper commonly grows to weigh a hundred pounds, surpassing all other nonmarine turtles of the United States in size if not in fierceness. A turtle's lack of teeth keeps its bite from being as bad as that of a well-toothed animal.

The lizards are about as harmless as the turtles. As already stated twice, only two of them have a venomous bite: the Gila monster of our Southwest and adjacent Mexico, and its close relative, the Mexican beaded lizard. Grooved rather than hollow teeth of the lower jaw make way for the venom but do not do so very effectively. As if to compensate, these large lizards have a strong venom and the nasty habit of chewing and hanging on. The biggest of all the lizards, the monitors, are powerful enough and have plenty of teeth, but happen to be bluffers rather than biters. The almost complete harmlessness of lizards as a group has not prevented a firm belief in their venomous nature from spreading around the world. How wrong we humans can be sometimes!

No crocodilian is venomous, and even some of the large kinds are inoffensive. The American alligator is an example of a big crocodilian little feared by those familiar with its habits. A female guarding her nest will attempt to chase away even a man; since her speed is not great, an active man has little to fear. The chance of being attacked by any but a brooding 'gator is less than one in a hundred. The American crocodile is relatively fierce and should be left strictly alone. Since the range of this reptile barely reaches the United States (southern tip of Florida), we are almost free from dangerous crocodilians. In Asia and Africa, some of the larger kinds of crocodilians may, under special conditions, become man-eaters. For sheer fighting ability the ferocious crocodilians far surpass the other reptiles. This is because of their skill in making a powerful tail and huge, well-toothed jaws co-operate to the disadvantage of the foe.

No matter how much you like snakes there is no denying the fact that many of them are dangerous. These dangerous snakes may be divided into the very small group of huge constrictors (boas and pythons) and the large group of venomous snakes. None of the constrictors is a man-eater, although any that grows to be longer than fifteen feet may be rated as dangerous. Even these do not attack man and have to be all but stepped on or picked up before becoming dangerous. Only two (boa constrictor and anaconda) species are found in the New World, and these live in or very near its tropics. Neither

[A] *Snake stings frog.*

[B] *Snake bites mouse.*

[C] *Hoop-snake catches and stings man.*

TRUE OR FALSE

[ANSWERS ON PAGE 96]

[D] *Milk snake milks cow.*

[E] *Snake trails squirrel.*

[F] *Puff adder's breath kills raccoon.*

[G] *Cobra "spits" at man.*

TRUE OR FALSE
[ANSWERS ON PAGE 96]

[H] *Cobra charms bird.*

[I] *Music charms cobra.*

[J] *Gila monster poisons spotted skunk.*

[K] *Man injured by monitor's tail.*

occurs in the United States. Every big land area of the Old World tropics has at least one but never more than a few large constrictors, which may range somewhat beyond the actual limits of the tropical zone. Oddly enough, these constrictors are dangerous because of their bite; they defend themselves with their jaws, saving their powers of constriction for prey. This does not mean that if you actually seized a very large one it would not wrap around you and squeeze you a bit out of shape; small to medium-sized individuals could do little damage this way.

ANSWERS TO TRUE OR FALSE PICTURES

[SEE PRECEDING PAGES]

[A] FALSE. *The tongue of a snake never injures either enemy or prey.*

[B] TRUE. *Snakes bite with fangs and teeth.*

[C] FALSE. *No snake either rolls about like a hoop or stings with the tail.*

[D] FALSE. *Neither our milk snake nor any other snake gets milk from a cow.*

[E] TRUE. *Snakes trail prey.*

[F] FALSE. *Hognose snakes ("puff adders") do not have poisonous breath.*

[G] TRUE. *Some cobras eject venom through specially constructed fangs (top, right).*

[H] FALSE. *Snakes do not charm birds.*

[I] FALSE. *Snakes are deaf.*

[J] TRUE. *The Gila monster and its close cousin are the only venomous lizards.*

[K] FALSE. *Monitors may lash with their tails, but cannot do so hard enough to cause injury.*

The venomous species are found throughout the snake-inhabited parts of the world, and may be common even outside of the tropical zone. They inject venom with a pair of big teeth or fangs that are formed essentially like a hypodermic needle (see last paragraph of this chapter). The venom comes from glands, one in either side of the head. Neither tongue nor tail ever has anything to do with getting venom into you.

This venom is really a special kind of saliva that probably was developed chiefly to help the snake get food. The venom has two major effects. It damages parts of the blood and the tiniest blood vessels, and it stops breathing and heart action by paralyzing big nerves. Damage to blood and blood vessels centers at the site of the bite and causes great swelling. In general, viper venom is the type that produces such local effects. The nerve-affecting type is, for the most part, injected by coral snakes, cobras, and their relatives. I have given a highly simplified account; snake venoms and their effects are extremely complex. Though thousands of technical papers have already been written on these venoms, we still know little about most of them. There is no general agreement on the proper treatment of snakebite.

Although the venoms cannot be sharply separated by their effects, the biting mechanisms are of two distinct types. One of these is found in the vipers, the other in the coral snakes, cobras, and their allies. The vipers have by far the better of the two. Their fangs are large and made like the hypodermic needle. In fact, they are so large that the jaws cannot be shut while the fangs are erect. This means that they have to be folded inward and upward against the roof of the mouth. For the development of this fine mechanism, great changes had to take place in the bones of each upper half-jaw. You can easily see that a long bone full of teeth cannot be rotated. (Compare the description of swallowing on page 22.) This difficulty was overcome by a shortening of each jaw and a reduction in the number of teeth to a single large one, the fang. The bone remained as a mere base or pedestal for the fang; such a "nubbin" is easily rotated and the fang of course moves with it.

The cobras, coral snakes, and their allies have fangs short enough to remain erect when the mouth is closed; they cannot be folded back because the bone holding them is not short enough to be fully rotated. They are not the perfect, freely movable, hypodermic-needlelike teeth of the vipers, neither do they have merely a lengthwise groove for venom conduction, as is often stated without basis in fact. It is clear that these fangs are not such good injectors of venom as are the perfect ones of the vipers. In addition to having a better mechanism, the vipers bite faster and more effectively. The cobras merely jab clumsily with raised head and neck; many coral snakes bite only at very close range, so close that they are not dangerous until stepped on or picked up. The viper usually bends its forward part into S-shaped loops, and strikes farther than the cobra.

Tests have shown that the viper's strike is not nearly as fast as was once supposed; yet it is too fast for most enemies and prey. The speed of the viper's strike (seven and a quarter feet per second in one rattler) is nothing compared to the speed of a bullet, and is even far less than that of a well-pitched baseball or well-served tennis ball.

In many parts of the world there are snakes with short, rigid, grooved fangs far back in the upper jaw. The vast majority of these rear-fanged snakes are harmless to man, and, therefore, I have left them out of the preceding account. It must be admitted that one of them, the boomslang of Africa, is truly dangerous to man; a few of the other large ones are able to inflict slight damage. The five rear-fanged snakes of the United States that reach appreciable size (up to three and a half feet in total length) are found only from southern Texas westward through southern California. None of them is to be feared, although it would not be wise to allow a large individual to chew a finger.

Finding Reptiles

AS a boy in northeastern Georgia, I used to read accounts of wonderful reptile hunts in our southern lowlands, and then go out to try my hand. I was lucky to find even one snake in a day's hunt. That was nothing compared with those exciting accounts. I then thought that I just did not know how to find snakes. Eventually I worked out the method of wading up small streams during the middle of a sunny day, and only in this way was I sure of catching a few snakes on every trip. It happens that two species of water snakes live in those streams, and both of them have the habit of sunning over the water on logs, bushes, or piles of brush. My experience illustrates some important facts about finding reptiles, or any other animals for that matter.

It is important to remember that reptiles are by no means evenly spread out over the suitable parts of the continents. My trouble was not so much an inability to hunt well as it was that reptiles are not nearly as com-

mon in the foothills of northern Georgia as they are in
its southern lowlands. Not only are more species found
in the latter, but also more individuals of many of these
species. In some areas of this earth you can scarcely take
a short walk without encountering several reptiles; in
other places you may search in vain for hours. By and
large, reptiles are more easily found in temperate regions
than in tropical forests. Such forests harbor plenty of
reptiles, but they are unbelievably hard to see because
they are so well hidden.

The second thing to remember is that very few reptiles
are broadcast over any region; each kind, as a rule, has

Success for the hunters. The snake will soon be in the bag.

its special haunt, niche, or habitat, whichever you wish
to call it. On the farms over which I roamed in Georgia
you hunted water snakes in streams because it was a
waste of time to look for them anywhere else. If there
had been ponds or other bodies of water, the snakes
would have been in them, too. This shows what is meant
by niche or habitat, and just how specific it can be. You
should find the habitat before starting to search for the
reptile. The name of an animal often helps: water snake
and canebrake rattlesnake, for examples. Habitats are
endless in variety. A very uniform region such as a dry
grassy plain clearly offers less variety than does one with
high as well as low vegetation and different elevations;
the latter is almost sure to harbor many more species.
It is remarkable that you can pick out an area in Ala-
bama and a similar one at the same latitude in China,
let us say, and find about as many species of reptiles in
one as in the other. It seems that the reptiles have taken
comparable advantage of regions of similar latitudes in
different parts of the world, with more species in the
warmer latitudes than in the colder ones. The exception
would be distant islands of the oceans; these have been
cut off by water so long that relatively few animals have
been able to reach them.

The third thing to consider in searching for reptiles
is the daily cycle of activity. I found my snakes most
readily near the middle of a warm, sunny day. They
were then sunning themselves over the water; by cautiously approaching them I could often make a final dash
and grab one before it slid or dropped in. Wading up-
stream had two advantages: I did not muddy the water

ahead and I was often a little lower than the snake. It is as necessary to know the daily cycle of any animal as it is to recognize the exact type of country it lives in. Some reptiles are to be seen only during the day, others through the night, and still others at twilight and in the early hours of the night. Differences in degree of temperature change may force the same kind of reptile to follow two cycles. For example, if its range is big enough to include a desert as well as a rainy region, there will be one cycle for the desert, another for the rainy area; midday desert temperature is too high for reptile comfort, the midnight one too low. Between these extremes the suitable temperature will be found.

The proper time of the year is of course something else to think about in hunting reptiles. This question of seasonal activity has already been considered in the chapter on various habits, and therefore will not be dealt with here.

For ideal hunting, then, you must be in good country during the best season and know the habitats as well as the daily cycles of all local reptiles; going out and just poking around will not get results. Learning to find reptiles is quite as hard as learning to play baseball or any other complicated game. The thing you need most at the start is a good handbook, preferably one of the region in which you hunt. Not long ago such books were scarce but now several good ones are in print.

The books by the Conants and Stebbins in this short list will enable you to identify any reptile of the United States or Canada; the Conants' book includes only eastern species. The others will either help you with particular groups or give you valuable information on habits, habitats, and distribution.

CARR, ARCHIE: *Handbook of Turtles. The Turtles of the United States, Canada, and Baja California.* Ithaca, New York: Comstock Publishing Associates; 1952.

CONANT, ROGER and ISABELLE CONANT: *A Field Guide to Amphibians and Reptiles.* Boston: Houghton Mifflin Company; (In Press).

OLIVER, JAMES A.: *The Natural History of North American Amphibians and Reptiles.* Princeton, New Jersey: D. Van Nostrand Company; 1955.

POPE, CLIFFORD H.: *Snakes Alive and How They Live.* New York: The Viking Press; 1937.

POPE, CLIFFORD H.: *Turtles of the United States and Canada.* New York: Alfred A. Knopf; 1939.
(This book is much shorter than *Handbook of Turtles* by Archie Carr.)

SCHMIDT, KARL P. and D. DWIGHT DAVIS: *Field Book of Snakes of the United States and Canada.* New York: G. P. Putnam's Sons; 1941.

SMITH, HOBART M.: *Handbook of Lizards. Lizards of the United States and of Canada.* Ithaca, New York: Comstock Publishing Company; 1946.

STEBBINS, ROBERT C.: *Amphibians and Reptiles of Western North America.* New York: McGraw-Hill Book Company; 1954, or later edition.

Methods of hunting vary from place to place, from time to time, and from reptile to reptile. The simple habit of looking under things lying on the ground can be used to excellent advantage. The flatter the object and the longer it has been there, the better. I refer to logs, stones, and natural or man-made debris of all kinds. If the logs are rotten, look in as well as under them;

piles of rocks, old roofing, decaying shingles, thick brush, and other debris should be examined bit by bit, the work beginning at the edges. It need not be added that a light, short-handled farm implement such as a hoe, rake, pick, or mattock often comes in handy for the log and rock turner and the trash investigator. If the handle is long, the collector is kept too far away. The experienced reptile and amphibian collector turns things over in his sleep!

Among all the backboned animals, the reptiles and amphibians are perhaps the most easily caught. Birds fly too well, mammals are too agile and nearly all are active only at night, and fishes live in the wrong medium. To capture all of these you need special equipment such as guns, traps, and hooks. To find and catch most reptiles, all you need is a good pair of legs, sharp eyes, and some agility. There is always the problem of what to do with a live animal after it is caught. With a reptile, you need only to drop it in a bag and tie the mouth securely by wrapping a string around it. *Never* use a drawstring. The reptile will not smother any more than you will if you pull the covers over your head at night. Do not put the full bags in a sunny place for long, or in a cold place either. If you are hunting fairly large reptiles, a pair of gloves may make you feel a little safer. The bites of small reptiles need not be feared; they are far milder than those of other backboned animals. In my own case, just one, among hundreds of reptile bites, ever became infected, and that only slightly. Bites of small harmless snakes are remarkably painless because the needle-like teeth merely make pricks that soon disappear. I am assuming that you will not be capturing venomous snakes; this should be left to professionals and advanced students. It goes without saying that special devices are needed for catching and handling such snakes.

Reptiles as Pets

IT must be admitted from the start that a reptile does not make a companionable pet like a bird or mammal. If it did, we would surely have domestic reptiles. On the other hand, a reptile is very interesting as a pet because in behavior and habits it differs so much from us. When it comes to tameness, the reptile makes a good score; many of them become extremely docile and even like to be handled. Another point in the reptile's favor is the relatively small amount of care and attention that it requires. It may be left alone for days at a time without suffering from neglect.

Nearly every one of us has had experience with some mammal or bird, and therefore knows what to expect of one as a pet. It is only natural to think that the reptile will be just as alert and active; a little experience will show how wrong this thought is. The reptile not only reacts more slowly, but has fewer ways of letting you know how it feels. Imagine a snake changing the expression on its face. The first trouble usually comes at feeding time. The hungry cat or dog lets you know in many ways that it is hungry, whereas the reptile may show complete indifference to food for days or perhaps weeks on end. Even when willing to eat, a reptile may seem to be unable to find food placed near it. Sickness in a dog or cat can be detected at a glance; a reptile may be sick a long time before its owner discovers that anything is wrong.

Reptiles do not have to be fed as regularly or as often as do mammals and birds. Daily feeding is seldom necessary, and weekly or biweekly ones will often suffice. It is not unusual for a reptile to live a year without any food. As to temperature, it must be recalled that the cold-blooded animal is normally active only at high temperatures. These range from 72°F. to 80°F., or from ordinary room temperature to a few degrees above it. This same cold-bloodedness means that very high temperatures must also be strictly avoided. All reptiles will succumb to strong sunlight flooding their cages. Some direct sunlight is, however, good for them.

Turtles are without doubt the favorite reptile pets in the United States. With few exceptions these pets are infants, and, unfortunately, infant turtles are extremely hard to raise. The result is that nearly all of them slowly die from poor nourishment. They need a great deal of calcium in the diet, something not easy to supply. Sore eyes and soft shell are a sure sign of lack of proper food. (The hatchling's relatively soft shell quickly hardens with normal growth.) A turtle well past the infant stage makes a better pet by far. In spite of all I have said, it must be admitted that a few turtle fanciers, by herculean efforts, do get turtlets to grow normally. A recent letter describes a pet cooter that increased her weight from an ounce or less (hatchling with yolk sac still evident) to five pounds in a few days short of nineteen months; her carapace measured nine and a qaurter inches in a straight line.

A strictly land turtle can be kept in any dry place, or even allowed to roam about the house. A fenced-off section of the yard is more suitable as this allows it to dig. Water turtles should be kept in a clean tank in which there is about an equal amount of land and water.

Turtles vary in their food preferences. Chopped raw liver, lean beef, or fresh fish will do for food of the carnivorous species kept in the city. In the country, include more natural food such as worms, soft insect larvæ, and

Adult turtles, the easiest of reptiles to feed, are almost indestructible.

the like. Tender leaves of lettuce and other juicy plants will be relished by omnivorous kinds. If you insist on keeping infant turtles, mix their food with bone sawdust secured from a butcher, crushed backbones of fishes, or bonemeal. Slices of small minnows may be used. Concentrated or natural cod-liver oil should also be given with food. Two feedings a week will suffice, except in the case of the infants, which require more frequent ones.

Snakes rate next to turtles as our most popular reptile pets. Before considering the housing and feeding of snakes, I want to emphasize two things. First, never try to scare anyone with a snake. Doing so not only is poor propaganda for snakes in general, but may lead to serious consequences. It is courteous as well as prudent to ask how a visitor feels about snakes before even bringing one into view. Second, every snake is an escape artist. There are few owners who have not learned this by bitter experience. The rule is to make your pet twice as secure as you at first think necessary.

In handling a snake give it as much support as possible. Do not pick it up by head or tail but near the middle of the body, and at once put your hands and forearms under it for extensive contact. Snakes only a few inches long must never be held in your closed hand for more than a fraction of a minute. Ignorance of this rule may cause the death of a nice little pet.

Snakes live well in clean, simple boxes that need not measure more than twenty-four by fifteen by fifteen inches unless the inmates exceed five feet in length. Light and good ventilation, especially the latter, are important, but should not be provided by the use of wire screening, except perhaps on top. An active snake may rub its nose raw against wire, even if it is only on top. Plastic screening is not as rough, but it is hard to see through. The easiest way is to give light by glass, ventilation by scores of small holes (about half the diameter of a lead pencil) in one or both ends of the box; if bored from the outside, inside roughness must be carefully removed. The box must be kept dry even for water snakes. The water container should be fixed in place, or the snakes given a drink when outside the box. Many snakes like to hide under some flat object such as a piece of bark or wood. When a snake is about to shed, it has to have some heavy, rough object against which to rub the loose skin. First, the eyes become milky or bluish; they soon clear up and shedding takes place about two days later. If there is difficulty in shedding, a warm bath may help. A shed should come off in one piece or a few very large ones, not in bits.

Taking care of a snake is as easy as rolling off a log except for feeding. This is a problem because snakes are often poor feeders, and the rats and mice eaten by so many are not readily secured. The first difficulty may be overcome by being careful to select individuals that eat readily. The matter of getting food is simplified by inducing the pets to take raw lean beef. This may call for patience at first, though many snakes will succumb. It is not true that dead animals are never eaten; many snakes accept freshly killed rats or mice. The more ambitious owners can provide food most easily by keeping a pair of white rats. These will produce large litters of offspring that are a convenient size for small snakes. Those not used at once will rapidly grow to a size suitable for whatever snake is hungry. Weekly or biweekly feedings suffice; one very large meal may be all the food needed for a month or two, especially in winter.

There are various ways of coaxing snakes to eat. Peel up a bit of the skin of the dead rodent, or allow the snake to "discover" the prey, dead or alive, in a small, dark box or in a tube of convenient size.

The lizard most widely kept in this country is the American chameleon, which is really an anole. Unfortunately, this reptile usually survives only about as long as it can fast. This is because of the wide belief that the anole thrives on a diet of sugar and water. Nothing could be further from the truth. Water is not taken from a dish, but licked from foliage. The food should consist of living insects and the like; movement attracts the anole's attention. Houseflies can be used, although a pure diet of them is not advisable. It will not do to turn the insects loose in the cage and then leave; you must watch to be sure that they are eaten. Insects are masters at the art of escaping and hiding; many an anole has starved because its owner took too much for granted. Two or three feedings a week will suffice. Horned toads, which are really horned lizards, make attractive pets but do not live long. They are insectivorous. Lizards are varied in feeding and other habits, so it is impossible to give here adequate directions for their care. Few kinds are commonly used as pets in the United States.

Crocodilians are suitable pets only for the most ambitious keepers. This is, of course, because of their size. The hatchling alligator will soon outgrow ordinary quarters unless it is in bad condition, and who wants a pet that is not healthy! Moreover, the traffic in baby alligators, once a thriving business, is now largely illegal. Dealers have more or less managed to get around this difficulty by importing infant caimans from tropical America.

It must be admitted, however, that a healthy crocodilian sometimes makes an especially interesting and alert pet. Small aquatic animals are the natural food, but in the absence of these, liver, lean beef, or fish, all raw, will do. A little cod-liver oil and bone sawdust should be added, especially for the very young. A reluctant feeder can be coaxed by advancing the food, supported on a stick, from one side; crocodilians often seize prey by sideswipes. The aquarium should be at least as long as its inmate, well ventilated, and clean. A dry, sunny basking place should be provided. The water need be kept only deep enough for submergence; its best temperature is about 75° F.

Usefulness

REPTILES have always been useful to man in many ways, although their value to him has never compared with that of birds, mammals, and fishes. From the point of view of the reptile, this usefulness is of two widely differing kinds. One requires the destruction of the reptile (for its hide, let us say), the other, its protection (as a destroyer of rodents, for example). Man is realizing rather late that in wanton destruction of animals he is also a loser. Happily this realization may have come in time to prevent total loss of valuable creatures which are products of centuries of evolution. For instance, millions of American alligators were slaughtered by hide hunters or were sacrificed to the novelty trade before laws, only recently passed, gave some protection.

Among the few other protected species of the United States are the American crocodile, the wood turtle, the eastern box turtle, the American chameleon, and the Gila monster. The last is, indeed, our only venomous reptile that has ever been thus favored. Examples of

blindness equal to our neglect of the alligator could be cited from all parts of the world, and in most cases no saving step has been taken. It is left to the coming generation to stop this horrible waste.

Turtles are unfortunate in being the only reptiles that everyone eats without shame. Perhaps the green turtle, a widely distributed marine reptile, has been relished by more peoples than has any other backboned animal. It is probable that almost every kind of turtle has at one time or another satisfied the broad appetite of man. No such statement can be made about lizards or snakes. Crocodilians hardly make a fair comparison, because so few species exist. However, at one time or another, man has probably eaten all of them.

The foregoing statements may give the impression that almost every turtle is eaten wherever it lives, but such is not the case. Each country has its own ideas about what is especially good in the way of turtle meat. For example, among some forty species found in the United States and its coastal waters, only two marine and two nonmarine species have really hit the market. One of the latter, the diamondback terrapin, became so reduced in numbers and elevated in price that it lost favor. The other fresh-water kind, the snapping turtle, is the surprise package; few of us know that it is widely used as food. Only in the Philadelphia region is it generally advertised by restaurants. Softshell and certain other species often reach local markets and are considered more or less of a delicacy by many who catch them, but they cannot be rated with the big four. Thus we see that some 75 per cent of our turtles do not arouse our appetites.

Crawling up beaches to lay has been the most costly of all turtle habits. What could a human being enjoy more than hunting on moonlit beaches for eggs, especially when finding them takes little time or trouble. Through the ages man has dug up nests, and even today in at least one part of the world the digging is done on a scale that rates it as an important national industry. The turtles make it easy by coming out of the water in hordes. Thanks to our lack of foresight, such hordes are no longer seen on any of our beaches.

Just as turtle meat satisfies man's appetite, so does its shell gratify his sense of beauty. "Tortoise shell," the outermost layer of the hawkbill's back, is made into many handy as well as ornamental objects. This marine turtle is found around the world and has been used in the arts and crafts since ancient times. In recent years plastics have come to its rescue by competing heavily with tortoise shell.

All the important uses that we have found for turtles necessitate their destruction or injury. We must admire these reptiles for having such ability to survive in spite of this, and we wonder how many there would be if their flesh and eggs were poisonous to us.

Snakes make out better than turtles do; in serving man, the snake is not always sacrificed. Many snakes eat rodents, and rodents in turn are one of the farmer's great enemies. There can be no doubt that a few bullsnakes in a grainfield will account for hundreds of rodents, especially the nestlings. Since a little more than a third of the one hundred and fourteen species of the United States and Canada are rodent eating to some degree, it is readily seen that snakes constitute a great threat to rodent life. More than a few farmers know this and do not allow their snakes to be slaughtered.

Many persons will be surprised to learn that snakes have long been used to cure diseases as well as to satisfy the appetite. The history of western medicine is full of references to concoctions with at least some snake in them, and today snakes preserved whole in liquid are to be seen in countless drug shops of Asia and other parts of the Old World. In the United States, snake oil was once a favorite remedy for various aches and pains. The peddlers of this oil kept the price high, because, they rea-

Bullsnakes are great destroyers of rodents that are harmful to crops. A bullsnake may remove dirt from a rodent's tunnel (below, left), hold a victim against the side of a tunnel, or constrict two rodents at the same time. To handle two victims at once, the snake seizes one and then, by passing it rearward, makes room for the second.

soned, a great deal of rubbing was necessary for deep penetration, and the higher the price the greater the intensity of application. The oil at least kept the skin from getting chafed, and the massaging was surely beneficial.

Even recent medical research has disclosed uses for snakes. Their venom has proved to be of value in the treatment of several diseases, and it is also used in preparing antidotes (antivenins) for snakebite. It could, of course, be argued that I am not justified in mentioning the latter use here; the antivenins merely combat damage done by a snake to begin with.

It has been stated that "the poor" of some parts of the world eat snakes. This is a rank understatement; snake meat is widely relished, and you may, if you have the price, even buy it in the best delicatessen stores of this country. Perhaps the highest appreciation of snake was developed in the Canton region of China where several kinds have a true market value and are expertly prepared in many restaurants. This probably was not at first a Chinese habit but one inherited from the pre-Chinese peoples of the region. In several other parts of China I was able to buy large snakes at low prices, my only competitors being the few men who collected them for the medicine shops.

Snake and lizard skins, with their beautiful patterns, have been used for an unknown length of time. The heads of drums are often covered with lizard skin in the Old World, and snake skin is used there as well in the construction of other musical instruments. The modern market for lizard and snake hides is an outgrowth of this and many other older uses. The quality of snake and lizard hides is often so good that expensive products are made from them, such as shoes and pocketbooks. Commercial collecting of the larger reptiles of these groups has developed to a scale threatening the very existence of many species. Laws that will conserve the rapidly diminishing supply are greatly needed. Fortunately, the snakes of the United States are not large enough to be of real value, and only novelties are made of their skins. Our lizards have fared even better.

Some lizards of this country are known to do a great deal of good by killing insects that are harmful to agriculture. To be specific, I shall mention only the well-proved case of the destruction of beet leaf hoppers by Utah lizards. Animals that do harm in other ways are also eaten by lizards. Alligator lizards relish black widow spiders and, in Ceylon, a monitor is protected because it eats crabs that in turn weaken rice-field banks by burrowing into them.

The larger species of iguanas are to be found in markets throughout tropical America, where the meat is universally considered a great delicacy. Tourists are often shocked at the sight of iguanas tied by their own tendons. The toenails are twisted loose so that the tendons attached to them may be pulled out and used in tying the legs over the back. Bullfights, cock-fights, prize fights, and trussed-up iguanas are sights to which many travelers never become reconciled, and not without reason. Large lizards are eaten in many parts of the Old World. These reptiles are also used as medicine but not as much as are snakes. The reason for this difference is something to ponder over.

The use of American alligator hides and of crocodilian flesh has already been mentioned. Other crocodilians are persecuted because of their valuable skins. The eggs as well as the meat are considered a delicacy in some parts of the world. Proper conservation could have kept the crocodilians as a perpetual source of valuable leather. There is an international movement on foot to protect them.

Reptiles and Man

MAN is both attracted and repelled by reptiles. The modern American who shudders at the thought of a reptile, especially a snake, may be surprised to learn that human beings have long had great respect for these lowly creatures and have often thought of them with awe.

In the United States there are two remarkable cases in which snakes are used locally as religious symbols. One of these is old, the other new. The Hopi Indians of Arizona live in such a dry region that their very life depends directly on rain. Every year they gather to pray for it. The prayer is in the form of a highly stylized and complicated dance. Live snakes, many of them venomous, are carried about in the mouths of dancers who are dressed in elaborate costumes. Snakes are seen as messengers to the rain gods, the association being rain—lightning—sinuous shape—snake. But how do the Hopis manage to carry rattlesnakes about without falling victim to their deadly bites? Probably it is skill that saves the Hopis. Every snake man knows that even venomous species can be handled by the expert with slight danger. There is a bit of evidence that some Hopis, now at least, know how to remove the fangs so carefully that the snakes are not injured.

The relatively new use of snakes in religion is to be seen in the mountains of our Southeast, where free handling of copperheads and highly venomous rattlesnakes is considered a test of faith. Less than half a century old, this practice is founded on the Bible. It is stated in the Gospel according to Saint Mark that "In my name they shall take up serpents. . . ." (16: 17-18). These instructions were followed so literally that "snake handlers" were often severely bitten; state laws soon forbade their activities. Photographs prove beyond doubt that the members of the cult are deadly serious, and often wrap large snakes about the head and neck at the risk of suffering horribly if poisoned. Here we see something of great interest, the actual birth of a cult, and we get some clue as to how religions expand. The fact that snakes are used makes the cult of double interest to us.

In the ancient world, especially the countries around the Mediterranean Sea, the serpent held great power in the affairs of man. It was supposed to be able to heal diseases, prolong and even beget life. Moreover, it was considered very wise. In some myths it stood as the head of the human race. There is evidence that the name Eve is derived from that of the serpent. Apparently, the Israelites settled in a country where the serpent was a principal divinity. Their god considered it a dangerous rival and cursed it "above all cattle, and above every beast of the field" (Genesis 3: 14). Nevertheless, there

are Biblical references to the wisdom of the serpent and to its power to heal. The snake is referred to variously as "adder," "asp," and "viper" as well as the more usual "serpent." Saint Paul was bitten by a viper, and considered as a god by the "barbarians" when the bite failed to take effect (Acts 28: 3-6).

The serpent worship of the ancient Egyptians, Greeks, and Romans was inherited in modified form by the Europe of relatively recent times. Asklepios, a prince in northern Greece, became the god of medicine. This god in turn had become a substitute for the healing serpent. Today, Æsculapius (Romanization of Asklepios), the symbol of healing, is always shown with a serpent wound around his staff. This serpent is not an imaginary kind, but a species well known to science. In ancient Greece it was kept in temples, even given to babies as a living toy.

Snake worship in India has taken many forms, and survives today. Not only is the snake a healer, a restorer of life, and a guardian of houses and temples, but a divine protector of the owners and inmates. The most renowned relation of snake to man in India is on a somewhat lower level. I refer to the relation of snake charmers and their cobras. The practice of "charming" snakes provides a living for thousands of persons; sometimes whole bands of charmers wander about together. Performances are watched with as much interest by the local people as by tourists. Every charmer has a gourd flute, which may be highly ornamented, and two baskets, which he balances on a pole. When a lid is raised the head and neck of a cobra may come quickly into view. The performer then plays his flute, and the snake "dances" to the tune. Since snakes are deaf to sounds carried through the air, the cobra is merely moving in an effort to keep its attention on the swaying trunk of the man. An alarmed cobra holds the front part of the body erect, and is highly sensitive to movements that take place near it. These charmers earn a meager living by putting on shows, selling cures for snakebite, and offering to rid houses of snakes. The last they only appear to do, since the snakes are first carefully "planted."

It seems that human beings cannot make up their minds about snakes. In one place they are worshipped as gods, in another they are slaughtered without reason. It must be very confusing and frustrating to the poor serpent. Is he the wisest of all creatures, or only a menace? Perhaps it all goes back to the old belief that it takes a poison to counteract a poison. This, long thought to be pure superstition, is now known to contain a grain of truth. The modern antidote for snake venom, antivenin, is made from the blood of animals that have first been injected with venom.

The snakes have stolen the show in this chapter and deservedly so. No other reptiles have made such a deep impression on the mind of man, either now or in ancient times. But other reptiles enjoyed their share of respect. The turtle has already been mentioned. It may be added that the Greeks once held this reptile sacred, whereas the ancient Hindus conceived of the earth as a hemisphere resting on four elephants that in turn stood on a great turtle. Turning to the New World, we find that the Zuñi Indians of our Southwest have a turtle totem. This indicates a belief that some of the Zuñis are descended from

turtles and at death again become turtles. The crocodilians, with their limited distribution, have not had as
much opportunity to become objects of worship, but
crocodiles are big and formidable enough to command
respect. There is the tale of a furious war in ancient
Egypt started by the slaughter of a highly venerated
crocodile. A tribe of Madagascar believed that it was
descended from crocodiles. If a man were killed by a
crocodile, the tribesmen gathered at the site to demand
delivery of the guilty creature, which, of course, was not
made. Then a baited line was set, and the first crocodile
caught was formally sentenced to death and executed as
the culprit. The desire for vengeance satisfied, the body
of the unfortunate animal was given human burial rites.

The many dragons of the Old World seem to be
divided between those inspired by snakes and those re-
sembling lizards, or even crocodilians. In China, where
the dragon was seen chiefly as a benevolent being and
became the imperial symbol, it is suspiciously lizardlike
in form. Since the early Chinese came in contact with
their alligator long before they met the dragonlike monitors (huge lizards) of their extreme southern region, there
is some uncertainty as to the exact origin of this symbol.
However, the Chinese dragon was of vast importance
not only to the educated but to everyone. The digging of
a deep well was considered dangerous because a dragon
of the earth might be pricked and caused to move; this
in turn would make the earth quake. Before smiling at
such a fear, we should bring to mind equally fantastic
beliefs now held by us in spite of what science teaches.
We shall not have to think very long, either.

PART II
REPTILE
DISTRIBUTION

The United States, Canada, and the Mexican Highland

THE reptiles of the United States, Canada, and the *highland* of northern and central Mexico must be treated as a unit. This is because the species of these last two areas are either the same as those of our own country, or else are closely related. If you knew all of our species well, you would recognize every one found in Canada. In Mexico, it would be different. On the highland you would recognize many species, and the rest would strongly remind you of those at home; along nearly all of the Mexican coasts, which are *low*, you would find strange tropical species, and the farther south you went, the more of these you would find. A glance at a relief map will show you that those Mexican lowlands are continuous with the tropical ones of Central and South America. It is not surprising that the tropical species of reptiles range up those Mexican coasts but do not appear on the highland, where very different living conditions prevail—conditions which are, of course, much like those of the United States and southern Canada. Reptiles are all but unknown in northern Canada.

Now I want to state three things about this whole area: it is extensive, it is made up of many types of country, and it is temperate in climate. The small part, lying south of the Tropic of Cancer, is so high that tropical conditions do not prevail there. All of these factors are important to the reptiles. The great area and the varied types of country give room for many kinds, and the temperate climate makes them hibernate at least part of the year.

Another glance at a map, this time one of the world, will show that no other great temperate region is so nicely set off by itself. The narrowness and the physical geography of Mexico account for this. Of all the divisions of the world that we shall consider separately, the present one is the most uniform, and therefore has a reptile fauna all its own.

So much for broad generalizations and comparisons with other parts of the world. What about the area itself from the reptilian angle? In general, there is a sharp increase in number of species from north to south; I have already pointed out that reptiles barely reach northern Canada, and everyone knows they abound in our warm, low southeastern states. The high mountains and plateaus of western North America introduce complications. The climate of the highest mountains in the United States is much like that of northern Canada at sea level, and no one would expect to find reptiles at such heights. The reptile "ceiling" is about ten thousand feet in the northern part of the United States, near eleven thousand in the southern. Many peaks of the Rockies and the Sierras extend several thousand feet above these limits. Downward from the small but numerous reptile-free areas, the number of species rapidly increases, just as it does from north to south. The mountains of the eastern part of the country are not too high for reptiles.

The crocodilians of the part of North America under consideration are two in number: the American crocodile and the American alligator. This is not many, although it must be admitted that we have a good share of the twenty-three living species. The American crocodile is our one reptile that is dangerous because of its size, strength, and ferocity. The alligator is a shy creature that almost never attacks man except when man disturbs a nest being guarded by a female. The crocodile, in contrast, is aggressive, and must be carefully avoided. There is, however, little difficulty in avoiding crocodiles in the United States because they have been driven to the wildest parts of extreme southern Florida and even there they are rare and shy. This shyness is in contrast to their viciousness when captive, and leads to the conclusion that they were not always so shy in Florida. They once lived in the bays and salty river mouths along two-thirds of the eastern coast of that state; on the Gulf coast they ranged only a third as far northward. Try to imagine the southern half of Florida three or four hundred years ago, with alligators up to nineteen feet long so abundant that you could walk across some small rivers on their backs, and even larger crocodiles common on both coasts. A twelve-foot alligator is now rare, and crocodiles, if seen at all, are little larger.

The American alligator stands out as the one common crocodilian at home only in the temperate zone. The Chinese alligator also lived north of the tropics, but it is almost extinct and exists only as a remnant. So many of our alligators have been slaughtered that they are now rare or even absent from most of the area where once they thrived. This area was the coastal strip from North Carolina to Florida, all of Florida, and the Gulf coast through southern Mississippi. In Louisiana the area expanded to include almost all of that state, the Mississippi valley into northern Mississippi and southeastern Arkansas, and the lowlands of eastern Texas to extreme southeastern Oklahoma. Fortunately, some states have now passed laws to protect this valuable animal and save it from extinction.

"What is the difference between a crocodile and an alligator?" This question is commonly asked in the United States. I am never sure whether the puzzled person wants to know the difference between alligators and crocodiles in general, or that between our crocodile and our alligator. I usually guess that the latter is meant; nowhere else in the world would the question have much meaning, because only in this country have the ranges of these animals overlapped. If my guess is right, the answer is simple enough: the crocodile has the much narrower snout. Unfortunately, there are broad-snouted species of crocodiles in other parts of the world, and so this distinction does not always hold. However, in all crocodiles everywhere the fourth tooth of the lower jaw fits into a groove of the upper; in alligators this tooth slips into a socket of the upper. Since crocodilians attack with the mouth open, this difference is not very useful in the wilds. Even if you landed in the jaws of the reptile, you would not be able to tell!

As already explained, snakes, lizards, and crocodilians are more abundant in the tropics than in the more northern or southern parts of the world. Turtles, on the other hand, do not fit this pattern; they may be just as numerous in temperate as in tropical places. Our region, for example, harbors some 15 per cent of all turtle species, whereas we have only 5 or 6 per cent of either snakes or lizards. If you could go anywhere in the world to study turtles, your best choice would be either the eastern United States or southeastern Asia. The turtles are a relatively ancient group; we see today only the few species that managed to hang on here and there. The snakes and lizards are now flourishing, and, therefore, have uniform rather than spotty distributions.

In the United States turtles are far from evenly distributed. They shun the region of the Rocky Mountains and the territory to the west of them. Among a total of thirty-five species, only one, the western pond turtle, lives entirely within this large western section, a good third of the whole United States. One other gets noticeably into the section from the east and one from Mexico. What a contrast this is to the central and eastern United States with about thirty species. Florida alone boasts seventeen; New England, as far north as it is, has no fewer than thirteen. The sea turtles, which are more or less abundant along both coasts, have been omitted from this discussion because nearly all of them range around the world and do not belong to any one region.

The reason for this crowding of turtles into the central
and eastern United States is not hard to find. Ours is a
water-loving lot of turtles and nearly all of them live
where there is plenty of water. We have, to be exact, only
one type of turtle that never enters water. This type lives
in the southeastern lowlands, where it is known as the
gopher tortoise; in the southwestern deserts, where it is
called the desert tortoise; and in northeastern Mexico
and adjacent southern Texas, where it becomes the Texas
tortoise. In spite of all these names it may be one species
with three slightly different populations. The box turtles, though not closely related, are our only other land
turtles, and one of our two species of box turtles takes to
the water during dry spells.

So you see that nearly all of our turtles are partial to
water, the great majority being out-and-out aquatic
animals. Among these, only the softshell turtles, two in
number, look like aquatic animals to the untrained eye.
A softshell resembles a pancake with legs, tail, and long
neck. The feet are webbed, and the head ends in a long,
slender snout. The shell is flexible and covered with skin
rather than hard shields. The disposition is so bad that
you should pick up a softshell cautiously, unless it is
small. There are only three other types of water turtles:
the snappers, large and ferocious; the musk and mud
turtles, smaller and smelly; and a big array of twenty-one
species, many of which have beautiful patterns and make
nice pets. Nearly all the turtles sold in pet shops belong
to this great assortment, the largest of all turtle groups.
Its members are found around the world except for
Australia. They are called simply fresh-water turtles, a

rather indefinite name; no one has ever thought of a better common one. To science they are emydids.

As explained in the first chapter, lizards of the central and eastern United States are often confused with salamanders; in the eastern states, salamanders may even be the more numerous. Salamanders are nearly always called "wood," "water," or "spring" lizards, though I have never heard of lizards being called salamanders. But in the western states, where lizards truly abound, there is little confusion because salamanders are scarce except in small areas. All this means that, in contrast to salamanders and turtles, lizards are lovers of dry country. Arizona, for example, has more than twice as many lizards (thirty-five species) as Florida (fifteen species). The lizards did a still better job of staying out of water than the turtles did of getting into it. In all our North American area, big as it is, there is no truly aquatic lizard, and virtually none that ever enters water. From this you must not generalize for the whole world. Lizards here and there do depend on water in one way or another, although none is really marine, and few are very aquatic.

In dealing with the turtles and crocodilians of our area, I had no occasion to mention climbing. Who ever heard of a truly arboreal turtle or crocodilian? The latter are satisfied with the ground; turtles do no more than clamber onto bushes overhanging water, where they sun themselves. On the other hand, our lizards have made no real use of water, but they have carried the possibilities of climbing to a greater extent than any other reptiles. This is true of lizards all over the world. In our area most of the species climb, although not always into trees and bushes. Many of them run over rocks and up almost any vertical surface they can find in Nature; nor do they overlook man-made things such as houses, fences, posts, and the like.

Being great lovers of warm places, lizards are not found as far north as snakes and turtles, nor as high above sea level as snakes. Turtles are excessively rare in the Rocky Mountains where they ascend only to about six thousand feet. Lizards occur in these mountains some three thousand feet higher than this, and roughly two thousand feet lower than snakes. Lizards barely enter Canada and are even lacking in northern New England; a single kind, the five-lined skink, ranges into southern New England, and there it is rare. New Englanders just have to get along with almost no lizards, whereas the people of the Southwest see them everywhere. What I have said about our Southwest applies, of course, to the Mexican highland, which is a lizard heaven like Arizona and California.

When it comes to the actual species, I must admit that our lizards are multiform and confusing. Not only are many salamanders thought to be lizards, but lizards without legs are taken for snakes. The lizards have the distinction of being our only confusing reptiles. Then, too, the species are numerous: about eighty in the United States and Canada and a great many others on the highland of Mexico.

Among those of this country and Canada, five lack limbs entirely and one has four tiny legs, which might easily be overlooked. Three of the five are the famous glass snakes. The tail is so long that the whole animal can be broken in two, as explained in the chapter on enemies and defense. At least one of the species of glass snakes is found in almost every part of the southeastern quarter of the United States; other legless lizards occur only in California and Florida. When, in one of these states, you catch a snakelike reptile that winks at you, you can be sure that it is a lizard; snakes do not have movable eyelids. If you handle your glass snake roughly, you may have to leave most of it behind. So many lizards have fragile tails that it is a good general rule never to use a lizard's tail as a handle.

About half of the lizards of the United States and Canada, taken as a unit, belong to one great family, the iguanas, or, to put it technically, the iguanids. The most familiar iguanids are the American chameleon, the collared lizard, the leopard lizard, the fringe-toed lizard, the earless lizards, the spiny lizards or swifts, the utas, and the horned toads. Then there is one other great family, the skinks, with seventeen species. Seven more families occur, but none with even half this number of species. The legless lizards we have just discussed belong to three of these seven families. The species with four tiny legs is a Florida reptile, the sand skink.

When it comes to the snakes of temperate North America there are three important things to keep in mind. First, in the United States and Canada alone, there are more species of snakes than there are species of any other group. In fact, snakes number about as many as do crocodilians, turtles, and lizards combined. (The marine reptiles, five turtles, are again left out.) The highland of Mexico has a fair number of snakes, although

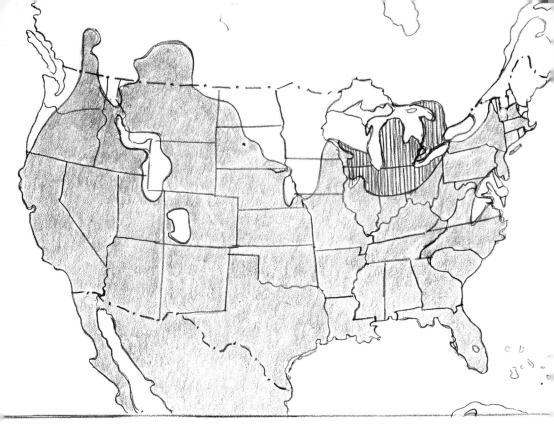

V E N O M O U S   S N A K E S   I N   T H E

RATTLESNAKES: *Taken together, our fifteen species of rattlers are widely distributed. The lined area (lower Michigan and adjoining regions) has only the massasauga, a small species whose bite is rarely fatal to adults. Though not so indicated on the map, this rattler also occurs along the southern shore of Lake Ontario.*

EASTERN CORAL SNAKE: *As indicated by the map, the eastern coral snake is a lowland species. The black snout and narrow yellow rings that are twice as numerous as either the black or red rings, distinguish it from strikingly similar harmless species. The small, rare Arizona coral snake (range not shown) is not a menace to man.*

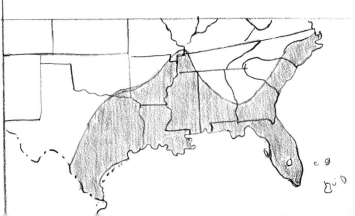

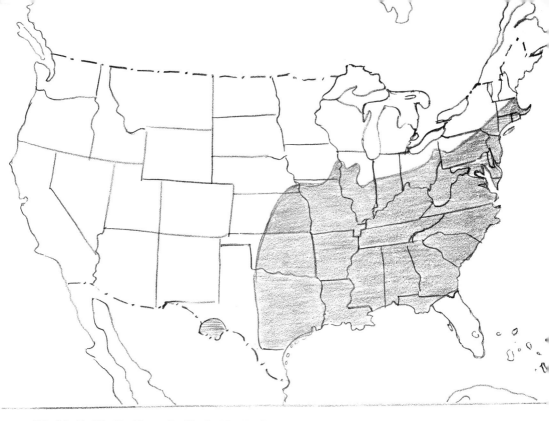

UNITED STATES AND CANADA

COPPERHEAD: *The copperhead is the most widely distributed of our three highly dangerous species of snakes without a rattle. The bite of the copperhead, though severe, is seldom fatal to adults.*

COTTONMOUTH: *All "water moccasins" living outside of the cottonmouth's range as shown at right are harmless water snakes. There are many kinds of these, but we have only one species of cottonmouth. This is often known as the water moccasin.*

here, as might be expected from the aridity, lizards are more numerous; turtles are few, crocodilians lacking. Second, snakes are found in every part of the United States except the small area that is more than ten thousand feet (in the north) or eleven thousand feet (in the south) above sea level. They thrive in the dry as well as in the well-watered regions. You will recall that the turtles cannot compare with this, and that the lizards fall noticeably short. Third, the snakes, like the turtles, make great use of pond, stream, and river; like the lizards, they use tree, bush, and other sites that call for climbing. It must be admitted, however, that the snakes of our North American region climb less than the lizards; in tropical forests snakes do much better.

It is little wonder that the rattlesnakes steal the show in our North American region. The early explorers and esttlers were duly surprised to find large and venomous snakes ending in a "bell" that they used as a warning. Nothing like it was known elsewhere. The "rattlesnake belt" lies where Mexico and the United States meet; in this highland area about half of the thirty known species occur, eleven of them in Arizona alone. Few species have wandered southward into tropical lowlands. The copperhead and the two cottonmouths (one of them Mexican) belong to the rattlesnake family, all being pit vipers and therefore dangerous. The only other dangerous snakes that live in Canada, the United States, and the highland of Mexico are a few coral snakes. Two of these are found north of Mexico; one, the Arizona coral snake, is too small and rare to be counted as a threat to man.

Having dealt with all our fearsome snakes, we can now '

turn to two surprise packages: our boas and blind (or worm-) snakes. Few of these live in our North American area, and those that do are found well west of the Mississippi River. To go into more detail, only two species of each family occur north of Mexico. For persons who think of boas as big snakes, our two, the rubber and rosy boas, will be disappointing. Only the latter grows to be as long as three feet. At first glance, our two blind snakes look like worms, and they have only the diameter of an unusually slender lead pencil (about three-sixteenths of an inch). Hatchlings are but three or four inches long, or about a third the length of the parents.

Although I have written about all of our venomous snakes and about these two surprise packages, the great majority of snakes are yet to come. Species of the one huge group of snakes, the colubrid family, are found around the world and occur abundantly in temperate North America. The total for this part of the world comes to more than a hundred species. None of these is notorious like the rattlesnakes, and only eight or nine groups of our colubrids are well known. The species of garter and water snakes are the most numerous and familiar of all. The garter snakes cover temperate North America like the dew, and range farther into Canada than any other snakes. Eleven kinds occur in the United States and Canada alone. The water snakes are generally distributed over the eastern half of our country. Some of the large and vicious species are everywhere confused with the cottonmouth, which is also widely known as a water moccasin. The racers and whipsnakes, the rat snakes, and the bullsnakes are perhaps the next most familiar. The species of these four groups help the farmer by eating large numbers of crop-destroying rodents. The king snakes, also widely distributed, are famous for their snake-eating habits. The story goes that they search out and devour venomous snakes; the truth is that they just like to eat any old snake, harmless or dangerous, that they can find.

South America, Tropical North America, and the West Indies

SINCE, as already explained, nearly all the Mexican coasts are tropical in climate, we must include them in our South American and tropical North American area. A glance at a map will show that the West Indies also belong here. Southern South America and the higher parts of the Andes are of course temperate, but we shall not set them off as a separate area. The animals of tropical America can be considered as good a unit for purposes of study as those of temperate North America.

The real contrast between the two areas lies in the different types of forests. The vast tropical rain forests that extend from Central America through the Amazon Basin are unmatched north of Central America. These jungles are inhabited by a great variety of animal life. The dense growth at the top of the jungle trees is a world all its own, a continuous mass of foliage in which thousands of animals live without ever going down to the floor. Our northern forests have no such second world.

When we compare the temperate and tropical New World areas, we find surprising similarities. One is the extent and location of warm deserts and regions of less extreme dryness. The South American deserts lie to the west like ours, and are flanked by less arid, elevated country that is about the same distance from the Equator as our own dry Southwest and the highland of northern Mexico. It must be admitted, however, that the South American deserts, unlike those of North America, extend into the tropics. Another similarity is the presence of open, somewhat flat grasslands in both temperate North and South America.

Because of their tropical location, number, and size you might expect the West Indies to have a lot of reptiles. If you went to the major islands you would see many lizards and some snakes, and this at first would be encouraging. But much hunting would soon show that there is little variety; you would be catching the same things over and over, and the different kinds would look much alike. Besides the lizards and snakes, you would find only one species of turtle and two of crocodilians, the rare Cuban and the widespread American crocodile. The most striking thing would be the total lack of venomous snakes in all of the islands except a few tiny ones in the extreme southeastern part near Trinidad. When you got to Trinidad all would change; that island, a mere chip off South America, is rich in reptile life of all kinds. It has not been separated long, and even now the waters poured against it by the great Orinoco keep it supplied with many South American animals hardy enough to get there on floating debris.

Tropical America is the land of crocodilians; more than a third of the species of the world, including all the caimans, live there. Caimans are cousins of the alligators, and only one of them, the black caiman, grows to be more than nine feet long. Africa has but four species of crocodilians, Asia six, and Australia two. Crocodilians are typically creatures of quiet tropical waters, especially of sluggish rivers and their mouths, so it is not surprising that they thrive in the Amazon and Orinoco basins. A single New World kind, the American crocodile, has taken to the sea and managed to settle on the larger West Indian Islands. It has, as already stated, even reached Florida. The tropical American crocodilians are not only numerous but large. The American and Orinoco crocodiles are the only species that probably grow to be twenty-three feet long; the gavial and the salt-water crocodile, both of the Asiatic region, fall short of this maximum by a foot or so. It must be remembered that, in these gigantic species, the average fully grown individual is only about half the length of the very largest.

A goodly variety of turtles live in tropical America; you could find greater variety only in southeastern Asia. There are three other things you should know about the turtles of the New World tropics. First, about a third of them belong to two great groups of water turtles with necks that are bent to the side when the turtle is resting or afraid. These are called side-necked and snake-necked turtles, and they live only in the southern hemisphere; you have to go to Africa, Madagascar, Australia, and New Guinea to see the cousins of the New World species. In some kinds the neck is so long that it has to be bent into a shape like an "S" to hide the head under the edge of the shell. These turtles are quite different from any you can see in the United States.

The second thing to remember is that our pancake-shaped softshell turtles are not found in tropical America, although they are common in Asia and Africa. In contrast to those side-necked and snake-necked turtles, the softshells are not found in either Australia or South America. There is a slight similarity between some of the side-necked turtles and the softshells. Both are flat and round in outline when you see them from above, but the likeness ends there. The shell of the side-necks is hard and stiff and the neck of the softshells is drawn straight back under the shell instead of being bent to one side or like an "S."

The third interesting item about these tropical turtles is the most striking of all. The Galápagos or Tortoise Islands (*galápago* meant tortoise to the Spanish, who discovered the islands early in the sixteenth century) lie six hundred miles west of Ecuador and on the Equator. Instead of being inhabited by man, they were the home of vast hordes of shelled giants. Many of these weighed hundreds of pounds, some more than five hundred. The early whalers soon learned to depend on them for fresh meat, and, as the years went by, the supply gave out. Today the Government of Ecuador protects the handful of survivors of the millions of giant tortoises that once swarmed over the islands. Oddly enough, no such giants live on South America itself. The two species of tortoises that do live there are by no means so large. You have to go all the way to the Seychelles and other small islands just east of Africa to find comparable giants, and that is a long way.

If you went to South and Central America looking for reptiles, the lizards would come to meet you, so to speak. They would be the only reptiles to be seen on all sides. You would have to go to special places to find turtles and crocodilians; tropical snakes, though all about, have an uncanny way of hiding. But lizards are as common in city parks and along well-used roads as they are anywhere, and many of them are by no means shy. You might find it hard to believe that actually there are nearly as many kinds of snakes as there are lizards.

The most notable thing about tropical American lizards is that almost half of them are iguanids. As already pointed out, the same is true for the United States. This does not mean that if you knew our lizards well you would recognize any tropical species; the relationship is not that close. But the tropical species would remind you, in a general way, of many of ours. If any species fooled you by looking just like one of our own, it would be an anole. This is because the American chameleon of the southeastern United States is an anole; it is merely the kind that has strayed farthest from the tropics where anoles swarm. The anoles often look so much alike that only an expert can tell one species from another. The number of species has been estimated as high as three hundred and fifty, and nearly all of them live in tropical America. In the West Indies alone there are almost a hundred.

In sharp contrast to the swarming anoles stands the common iguana. This species, with no very close cousin, is the giant among New World lizards; it is surpassed in length only by a few monitors, heavy-bodied Old World reptiles. The common iguana grows to be six feet seven inches long, and lives in jungles. There it may be seen diving from foliage overhanging water. Size and flesh with a delicate flavor combine to the disadvantage of this reptile. In tropical markets it is, as already explained, often offered for sale with the limbs tied up over the back. Lack of space makes it impossible even to attempt to describe the remaining tropical iguanids, fascinating as they are.

To the reptile specialist the outstanding lizards of South America are the teiids. The very fact that there is no common English name for them gives a clue to their range. They are almost entirely confined to tropical America. Anyone living in the southern two-thirds of the United States can get some idea of a teiid by looking at a racerunner or whiptail. Our racerunner and six species of whiptails belong to the one teiid lot that got so far north, the only one, in fact, that managed to invade the northern temperate region. In tropical America, the teiids, though far less numerous in species than the iguanids, are much more diverse—that is, there are more types of them than there are of iguanids, or any other lizard family for that matter. In spite of all this diversity, the teiids have never taken to the trees like the iguanids. A climbing teiid is a rarity, an iguana in a tree is a common sight. Many tiny teiids crawl about the forest floor and are rarely seen by man; others are large, though none rivals the common iguana in length. Excepting our racerunner and whiptails, the most familiar

Reptiles of northern South America: boa constrictor [A], South American tortoise [B], northern tegu [C], and spectacled caiman [D]. The snake has wrapped itself around the vine because the vine is too small to be climbed in the usual way.

[A]

[B]

[C]

[D]

teiids are the tegus. These South American giants are often two or three feet long, and may be seen in many zoos. The caiman lizard is a remarkable aquatic teiid that looks like a little crocodilian. It grows to be four feet long.

The only other large and important families of tropical American lizards are the geckos and the worm lizards. The former are, with few exceptions, climbing lizards with pads on the tips of the toes. They are more common in the Old than in the New World. No other lizards are so often carried about by ships. A few Old World species have been brought to the New World, and some New World kinds have been taken from one region to another. All New World geckos are small. The worm lizards are well named—they look and move much like worms, and, with few exceptions, lack legs. Some students even refuse to regard them as lizards at all. Worm lizards abound in tropical America, but are seldom seen because of their burrowing habits. About seventy species live in the New, somewhat fewer in the Old World.

The snakes found from the lowlands of Mexico southward into Argentina rival in number of species those living anywhere else. Southeastern Asia together with the East Indian Islands would be the chief competing place. It is probable that three times as many species live in a wide strip across South America as in a comparable strip across North America such as the United States. Brazil, slightly larger than the United States, is known to have only about twice as many species, but Brazil does not include the Andean highlands and the western coast, areas where the number of species would be especially great. Undoubtedly there are many snakes in tropical America that are yet to be discovered. This cannot be said about the United States.

All of the major groups of nonmarine snakes are plentiful in the New World tropics. We have space to give only a brief account of some of the important groups and a few spectacular species. Several of the latter are venomous snakes, and my account may make them seem to be more numerous than the harmless ones. This is by no means the case. It is just that the great array of harmless kinds (perhaps six-sevenths of all tropical American species) are too numerous to describe. Few have good English names and the vast majority belong to the one huge family of snakes (Colubridæ) found everywhere around the world both in tropical and temperate places. The hundreds of tropical American species of this family have made great use of every possible type of living quarters. Some live in water, others in or on the ground, and still others in trees and bushes. A few of the latter are so slender that you would take them for a thin vine.

The boa constrictor is by far the most famous snake of the American tropics. To many people this name stands for any gigantic snake. Actually, the boa constrictor is a definite species, though one of the lesser giants; it grows to be from ten to fifteen (rarely eighteen) feet long. The anaconda, a water-loving boa of our tropics, is truly *the* giant among New World snakes; it has a maximum length of at least twenty-eight feet. About two-thirds (some twenty-seven species) of all boas live in the region we are discussing, and they range in size downward from the anaconda and boa constrictor to midgets usually but eighteen inches long.

The pit vipers are the real snake threat in the New World tropics, and three kinds stand out among approximately fifty. These three are the bushmaster, the fer-de-lance, and the tropical rattlesnake or cascabel (*cascabel*, you will recall, means "bell" in Spanish). The first of these grows to be eleven or even twelve feet long, and has no rival in size among pit vipers. It is the only New World pit viper that lays eggs. Bushmasters, lovers of humid forests, hardly deserve their reputation for great ferocity. The fer-de-lance, with a maximum length only two feet less than that of the bushmaster, is a much greater threat to human peace of mind. It lives in almost every type of country and, literally as well as figuratively, thus comes into frequent contact with man. The cascabel, a large and highly dangerous creature, is the only rattlesnake that has spread itself over an appreciable area of the American tropics. It is found throughout their drier parts except the narrow strip of coast west of the Andes and, of course, the Andes themselves (which are not tropical).

More than forty close cousins of the two coral snakes of the United States are spread throughout the American tropics. Most of them are, like ours, brightly adorned with rings of red, yellow (or white), and black. However, in spite of having a very strong venom, these beautiful snakes are not highly dangerous to man—for three reasons. First, coral snakes have short fangs that will not go through leather or heavy clothing. Second, they do not strike out like vipers and are perfectly harmless except when stepped on or handled. Third, they are secretive, spending most of the time hidden. Need I add that they should *never* be handled by the novice?

Finally, I shall merely mention that numerous species of blind or worm-snakes are to be found in tropical America. These creatures look so much like earthworms that most of us would not even think of them as snakes. Their tongue, eyes, and dry, polished scales distinguish them. New World species, small and harmless, are especially varied and unusual in structure.

Europe

EUROPE is really part of one huge continent, Eurasia, and perhaps should not be considered here as a separate unit. I am setting it off because it is to a great extent a peninsula of Eurasia and extremely important as a major center of reptile and amphibian study.

Before taking up the reptile groups of Europe, I want to deal briefly with its climate and position as well as with the lack of snakes in Ireland. We read about the people of England enjoying a climate like that of our Southeast. Next we learn (with a bit of a shock) that London lies as near to the North Pole as does the northern tip of Newfoundland, whereas all of Ireland is farther north than that province of Canada. One of our earliest lessons in geography explains how an ocean current warms the British Isles. This same current makes it possible for both snakes and lizards of western Europe to live north of the Arctic Circle.

Everyone knows why Ireland has no snakes; St. Patrick, who was sent there in A.D. 432, drove them out. So runs the popular explanation. Science and history give a better one. The truth about St. Patrick and serpents is probably nothing more than that he forbade serpent worship because it did not fit into the teachings of Christianity. The belief that St. Patrick drove out the snakes themselves is just another bit of folklore flavored with a grain of truth. Science explains that Ireland has no snakes because, along with the rest of Europe, it was covered with ice not so long ago. At that time it, as well as Great Britain, was connected with the mainland; during the ice age the ocean level was lower. As the ice melted, the level of the sea rose and cut Ireland off before the snakes could reach it. Great Britain became an island soon after, but not before three kinds of snakes had arrived. It is even possible that some had managed to live in extreme southern England throughout the ice age.

It is not surprising that no crocodilians live in Europe; all of it lies well north of the Tropic of Cancer and even north of the range of the American alligator, the most northern of crocodilians. The turtles are anything but numerous and wide ranging. Five of the six species live in southern but not northern Europe, the sixth in southern and central Europe. Three of the five are land turtles, typical tortoises. Two of the three are the only turtles confined to Europe. This is a very small share of some two hundred and thirty species of the world. Australia, too, has a low count: fourteen species, ten of them found nowhere else. It must be understood that the sea turtles have been left out; all of those living in the Atlantic Ocean occur in the seas bathing European shores.

A glance at a list of the lizard families with European

species gives a false idea of the richness of the lizard fauna of Europe. A little study will show that only one of the seven families amounts to much there. The single true chameleon is a mere spill-over from Africa, where true chameleons abound. The two to six species in each of five other families are very poor samples of large families with more or less world-wide ranges; the few European species may be thought of as mere intrusions from Africa or Asia, and little better than the chameleon. As might be expected, the vast majority of the species are confined to the parts of Europe next to Africa and Asia.

The one lot that amounts to much numerically is the lacertid family. Lacertids are unknown in the New World, and we therefore have no good name for them. In Europe, on the contrary, about three-fifths of all lizards are lacertids. So common are they that most Europeans think of them merely as "lizards." They are found on all the British Isles and have even crossed the Arctic Circle in Scandinavia.

What I have said about the European lizards is essentially true of the snakes, except that two lots of snakes are well represented and widely distributed; these are the colubrids and the vipers. Almost two-thirds of the thirty-one species belong to the former, about one-third to the latter. This clearly does not leave many other species— actually, one worm- or blind snake and two sand boas. The lizard fauna is much the larger, since the number of species in the single big group of lizards approximates the whole lot of snakes.

Asia and the East Indian Islands

ASIA and the East Indian Islands, taken as a unit, form the largest of our six divisions of the reptile world. The total area of this major unit is, in fact, twice that of *all* North America. North America and Asia have something in common that makes them different from the other continents—the northern part of each is a vast, cold, reptile-free region. Asia is alone among the six divisions of reptile distribution in having an east-west barrier making a sharp dividing line between its southern (chiefly tropical) and central (temperate) sections. This barrier, the cold Tibetan highland, is often and aptly called "The Roof of the World." To the west of this barrier stretches an extensive arid region, elevated and more or less mountainous, which is by no means reptile free, thanks to a relatively high temperature. Although the section east of Tibet has no barrier, there is, oddly enough, a very sudden decrease in richness of reptile life at about the same latitude as that caused by Tibet. The Yangtze River flows eastward through this section. The dry climate of northern China and the intense cultivation that has gone on there for thousands of years probably help to account for this surprising decrease. From West Pakistan and India eastward to the China Sea lies the reptile heaven of Asia. Marked variation in altitude and a hot to warm climate combine to make this southern extremity of Asia the home of a goodly share of all reptile life.

The East Indian Islands are but a continuation of this reptile heaven with the Malay Peninsula as a link. The animals of this peninsula are, indeed, much more like those of the islands than they are like those of the rest of Asia. The Philippine Islands, but not New Guinea, make up a part of the division of the world under consideration.

The reptile picture of Asia, even without the East Indian Islands, is certainly the most complex on earth. In spite of the continent's great size, its reptile-rich area is not much bigger than that which is reptile free. The former, that reptile heaven, is barely a fifth of the continent's total area. The great southwestern deserts have their own peculiar types of reptiles often related to African species. The reptiles of central Asia are much like those of Europe and have distant relationship with North American types. The cold Tibetan highland lies nearer to the Equator than any other large area so devoid of reptiles. One more thing should be pointed out: the sudden rise from the steaming plains of northeastern India to the Tibetan highland makes a narrow strip of rugged country ideally suited to variety of reptile life;

here is the reptile lover's finest hunting ground in all of Asia.

This huge continent, with six species of crocodilians, ranks below tropical America (with eight species) and above Africa (with four). The total distribution of the crocodilians of Asia is not wide as in Africa and South America, but limited, as in North America and Australia. In Asia, the limitation is to that reptile-rich southeastern fifth, 'which reminds us of the limitation of our own alligator and crocodile. Three of the six Asiatic crocodilians have managed to get into the East Indian Islands, while a seventh species is found in the Philippine Islands.

As compared to those of tropical America, the crocodilians of Asia make up in variety what they lack in number of species. In fact, all of the three family groups of the world are represented. Let us begin with the alligator of the lower Yangtze valley, a reptile on the verge of extermination. Its single close relative is our own alligator, which has also suffered at the hands of man. The gavial of East Pakistan and adjacent regions is the most unusual of crocodilians. The snout is a remarkably slender fish-catcher, poorly fitted to the capture of big prey. The human ornaments that have been found in gavial stomachs certainly were swallowed with parts of corpses. Still another fish-eating crocodilian with the same type of snout is found on the Malay Peninsula. In spite of the shape of the snout, this odd reptile, known as the "false gavial," is not really a gavial but a crocodile with a narrow snout. Asia's three other crocodilians are run-of-the-mill crocodiles; two of them, the mugger

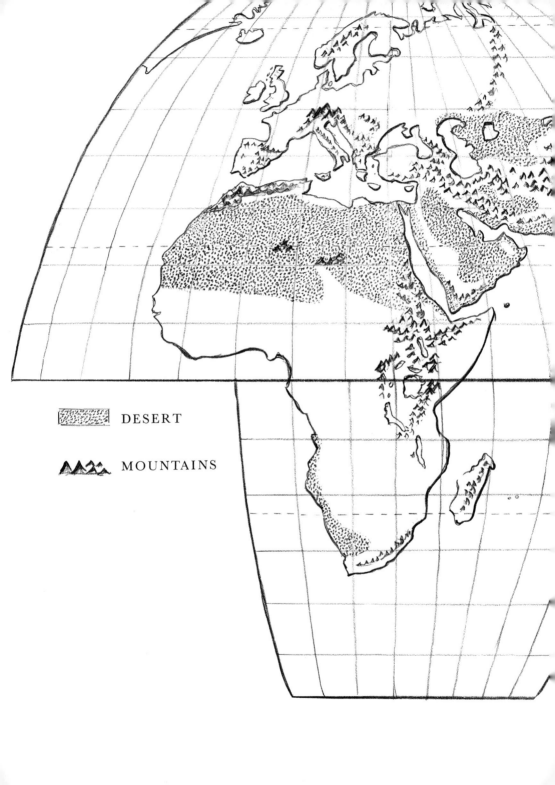

DESERT

MOUNTAINS

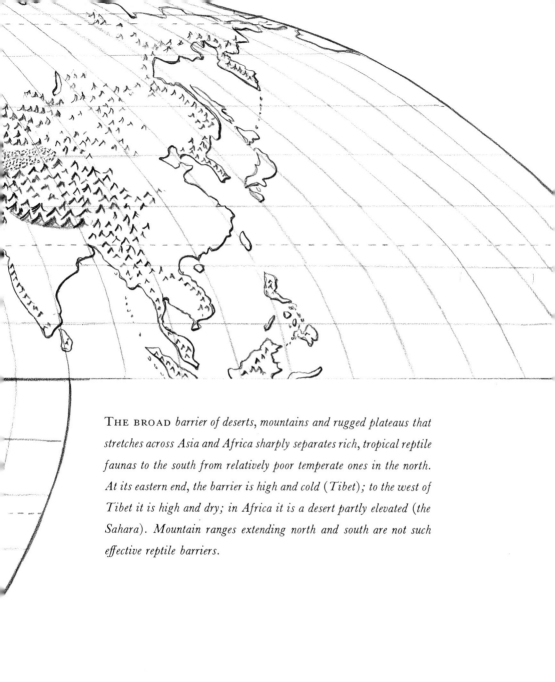

THE BROAD *barrier of deserts, mountains and rugged plateaus that stretches across Asia and Africa sharply separates rich, tropical reptile faunas to the south from relatively poor temperate ones in the north. At its eastern end, the barrier is high and cold (Tibet); to the west of Tibet it is high and dry; in Africa it is a desert partly elevated (the Sahara). Mountain ranges extending north and south are not such effective reptile barriers.*

or marsh and the salt-water crocodiles, are widely distributed.

Asia and the East Indian Islands have just about
cornered the turtle market. Their grand total of sixty-six
nonmarine species amounts to nearly a third of all such
turtles known to science. Since only two of the sixty-six
are found in the East Indian Islands alone, the picture
is changed little if we consider Asia by itself. When we
analyze these Asiatic turtles we find that almost two-
thirds of the species belong to the great family of fresh-
water turtles (emydids) so common in temperate North
America. In short, the turtles of Asia often remind us
strongly of our own. Ours are, however, much less varied
and only a little more than half as numerous in species. The
musk and mud and the great snapping turtles, so familiar
in the United States, are entirely lacking in Asia. To
somewhat offset this, Asia has a remarkable variety of
those strange creatures, the softshell turtles. This array of
four-legged, long-necked pancakes puts our two species,
which are much alike, to shame. One of the fourteen
Asiatic species has flaps on the rear of the lower shell and
a movable part at its front. When head and limbs are
drawn in, the flaps and the movable part are raised to
meet the lowered edges of the upper shell. Here we have
a softshell that can close up a flexible shell and do so as
tightly as our box turtles close their hard ones.

In addition to the fresh-water and softshell families,
Asia has nine species of typical tortoises. One of these
reaches the respectable length of eighteen inches (upper
shell). Finally, there is the ridiculous big-headed turtle
with a flattened shell, huge head, sharp beak, and long

tail. It lives in mountain streams, an unusual place for a turtle. This creature stands alone in a family; it has no close relatives.

Lizards have done very well in Asia and the East Indian Islands, where they are the most conspicuous and generally distributed of reptiles. They range farther north in Asia itself than any other reptiles. Lizards thrive in arid regions, and, as I have already pointed out, Asia has plenty of these. The snakes, of course, come second in numbers; actually there are more species of snakes than of lizards in the tropical southeastern section and the East Indian Islands, but the lizards are ahead in Asia's vast deserts and bordering dry areas. In spite of this, it is more difficult to write about the lizards because almost none of them is known in our part of the world; nothing familiar can be used for comparison. Among the snakes there are the vipers, the pythons (so much like our boas), and the cobras (relatives of our coral snakes). The average person would find it hard to name a single Asiatic lizard.

Let us take the skinks, the most numerous and widely distributed of all lizards. The expert can turn up one of these smooth-scaled, agile reptiles in nearly every part of the United States except the extreme Northeast, yet how many of us can tell a skink when we see it? In Asia and the East Indian Islands skinks outnumber all other lizards by species count, and in many places the individuals may be unbelievably abundant. Next come the agamids, Old World lizards without a well-known name in English. The flying dragons are little agamids that sail from tree to tree on winglike extensions of the skin. No other living lizards have taken to the air. In Asia and the East Indian Islands there are climbing as well as ground agamids. Many of them are extremely odd in appearance. They display spines on body or tail, crests, and other decorations that make them look like something out of this world. One of them even lays an egg that is shaped like a spindle, big in the middle and pointed at either end. The great family of the United States, the iguanids, is closely related to the agamids, although, among our iguanids, only the horned toads rival any of the odd agamids in looks. The third and last great group, the geckos, has almost as many species in Asia and the East Indian Islands as the agamid family has. Geckos are the only lizards with a voice, and they have carried the business of climbing to its highest state among lizards. The toes of many have not only big pads but claws that can be drawn in like those of a cat.

The rest of the Asiatic lizards worth mentioning belong to three lots. First, the lacertids, relatives of the lizards so common in Europe. Lacertids are found all over the reptile country of Asia, with a sharp decrease in number of species from northwest to southeast; a single species reaches the East Indian Islands, where agamids abound. Second, the monitors, the giants among lizards. The true home of monitors, lizards that resemble the mythical Chinese dragon, extends from the deserts of southwestern Asia eastward and southeastward through Australia. The latter has twelve species, whereas Asia and the East Indian Islands together have thirteen. Africa has only three species. Third, a real surprise, a

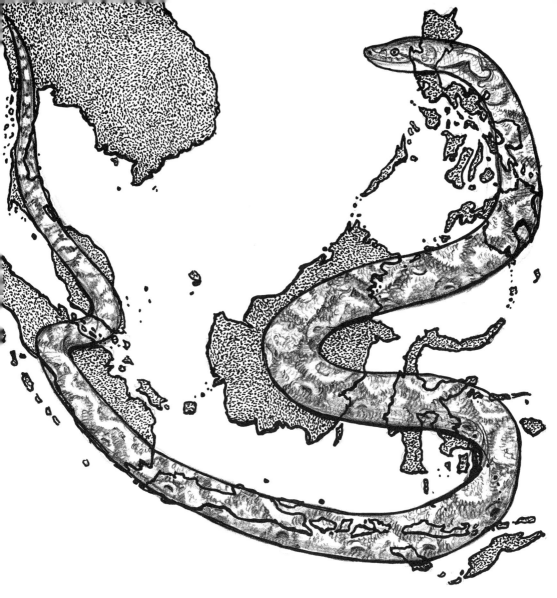

The reticulate python is used here as a symbol of the close relationship between the reptiles of the Malay Peninsula (covered by python's tail) and those of the East Indian Islands and the Philippines. The large island in the middle of the illustration is Borneo.

few species of legless or nearly legless lizards, extremely close relatives of our own glass snakes.

Asia and the East Indian Islands run away with highest honors when it comes to variety of snakes. Every family as well as almost every subfamily is represented there, and several such groups are all but confined to this geographical division. The freshwater snakes (Homalopsinæ, not to be confused with ordinary water snakes) and the wart snakes barely spill over into northern Australia. Only one among some fifty species of sea snakes has spread its range far beyond the Asiatic and Island region. The peculiar shield-tailed snakes, some of which have tails ending in a flat disc set at an angle to the axis of the body, are found only in the Indian Peninsula and on Ceylon. These reptiles appear to be the true burrowers among snakes. When it comes to total counts, we find that southeastern Asia has some four hundred species, the East Indian Islands about three hundred and fifty. Since many species live in both areas, we cannot get a true total for the two places by combining these figures. Making allowance for this duplication and adding a hundred species for central and western Asia, we grant Asia and the East Indian Islands a total of eight hundred, or nearly a third of the snake species of the world. This is less surprising when we realize that, in area, Asia and the East Indian Islands equal approximately half of our other five divisions of the world combined.

Among Old World snakes, the Indian cobra perhaps stands out as the most familiar, largely because of tourist and newspaper accounts of snake charmers as well as Kipling's famous story of the snake-baiting mongoose,

Rikki-tikki-tavi. Unfortunately, most such romantic stories are at variance with truth, and must be exploded. The cobras are not charmed, and the mongoose is not the sworn enemy of the cobra. The grain of truth in Kipling is that some mongooses, like many other mammals, do occasionally eat snakes, and mongooses will fight cobras. (Compare the remarks on page 70.)

The other famous Asiatic snakes are the great pythons so often seen in circuses. There is nothing misleading here; the reticulate python, probably the longest of snakes, deserves its name as a giant, and the Indian python, though smaller, reaches the great length of twenty feet. But continuing this species-by-species description of Asiatic snakes would take up far too much space. The reader will just have to imagine an endless procession, snakes of all sizes, hues, and shapes moving in a sinuous and colorful parade. This may sound like a nightmare to some readers, but to those with a deep appreciation of grace in movement and beauty in design, it will, indeed, be a pleasure.

Africa and Madagascar

TO MANY of us, Africa is the strangest and most exciting of continents. This is largely due to its animal life. But before we consider this fascinating subject, let us see how Africa compares in general with other continents. Though nearly twice the size of South America, it is a great deal smaller than Asia. Africa and South America are the only continents with extensive forests straddling the Equator. Every continent but Europe has its great warm desert, but the deserts that stretch across northern Africa and into the heart of Asia put all others to shame. These deserts and the dry regions connected with them link the fauna and flora of Africa to that of Asia. Finally, Africa is the one large continent that, from tip to tip, is well suited for reptile life.

When it comes to topography, Africa is much like North America, with the important difference that Africa's highest mountains are located in the tropics. There reptiles can make best use of them. Comparable altitudes are reached by African mountains and our own.

The extremes are remarkably close: Mount McKinley (20,300 feet) is a thousand feet higher than Mount Kilimanjaro (19,324 feet). But Mount Kilimanjaro raises its snow-white head only two hundred and twenty-five miles south of the Equator. Mount Kenya, just two thousand two hundred and eighty-four feet lower, all but rests on the Equator. Some Andean peaks, but no others anywhere, can match these two for high altitudes at low latitude. Many Rocky Mountain peaks are between fourteen and fourteen thousand five hundred feet in altitude, but none exceeds the last figure. The highest peak of the United States proper is Mount Whitney (14,496 feet) and located in the Sierra Nevadas.

From a strictly scientific point of view, the northern fringe of Africa should be separated from the rest of that continent and treated as a part of Europe. This is because so many European species of animals either reach this fringe or have very close cousins there. In short, the Mediterranean Sea is not the barrier to animal life that one might expect it to be. I need not add that the Sahara Desert keeps these European species and their cousins from getting far into Africa. Central Africa, which is tropical, has just about everything to offer reptile life: low as well as slightly elevated rain forests, dry highlands, towering mountains, rivers, and even great lakes. Here thrives a varied reptile fauna in the class with those of southeastern Asia and northern South America.

Madagascar lies off the southeastern coast of Africa, and is almost as big as Arizona and New Mexico taken together. With such size, a good range of altitude, and a location that is about as close to the Equator as is southern Mexico, Madagascar should make a fine home for animal life. But this island proves to be more than just a place with a profusion of animals; it is the world's greatest refuge of odd types. In many cases these types have no relatives in the part of Africa that lies only a few hundred miles away (two hundred and fifty miles at the nearest point). One thing is clear: Africa and Madagascar have been separated for a long time; there is even a belief that they were never connected. Just how some of Madagascar's oddities got there is still a mystery.

You have probably read stories about little birds cleaning the teeth of Nile crocodiles asleep with their mouths open. Herodotus wrote about this four and a half centuries before the Christian era. That the bird cleans the teeth of this great reptile or warns it of coming danger is pure myth. This crocodilian, one of the larger species (maximum length sixteen feet), is found over nearly all of Africa except the northern deserts. Nile crocodiles sometimes attack and kill human beings. In spite of this, they have long been extremely useful to man. Not only are the flesh and eggs eaten, but the hide, scales, and musk are used in various ways. This is one of those African species that crossed the narrow Mozambique Channel and found a haven; it was once called the most abundant backboned animal on Madagascar!

None of the other three African crocodilians can compare with the Nile crocodile in either fame, size, or width of range. However, each has its own points of special interest. The African slender-snouted crocodile grows to be only five to eight feet long, and is one of the four crocodilians with a very slender snout of the fish-catching type. It lives only in western central Africa. Then, in the Congo Basin and the country just west of it, there dwells a rare midget, the smallest of crocodilians. It grows to be only forty-five inches long at the most and is known as the Congo dwarf crocodile.

In spite of Africa's great size, it has fewer species of turtles than does temperate North America. When the species of these two geographical divisions are compared, interesting differences as well as likenesses come to light. Africa boasts a great many side-necked turtles, whereas we have none. (Recall that the rest of the side-necked turtles live in South America.) We have two snappers, and a lot of musk and mud turtles; Africa lacks all of these. Then, too, our great group of fresh-water turtles is unknown in 99 per cent of Africa; the few that are there are merely a tiny spill-over from Europe, and are confined to that northern fringe of Africa already discussed. Just to turn things around, as it were, the huge family of true tortoises represented in temperate North America only by the gopher tortoise (and its two cousins) makes up some two-thirds of the whole African turtle fauna. Finally, Africa has the edge on us with five against our two soft-shells. Notice that where we are weak, Africa is strong, and vice versa; we have two families that they lack and they have one that is missing here.

Madagascar has been left out of the above paragraph; all but two of its six species of turtles are true tortoises found nowhere else. The two that are not true tortoises belong to the family of side-necked turtles and one of the two is found only on Madagascar.

Although true tortoises are found in five of our six

major divisions of the world, it is in Africa and on nearby islands that they really come into their own. Here there are midgets and giants, high-shelled and flat-shelled species, tortoises with hinged upper shells, others with all-but-boneless flexible shells, and still others in which each shield rises to form a little pyramid. The tortoises with a flexible shell live in rocky country. Sometimes they protect themselves by crawling into crevices and filling the lungs with air. No other tortoise (or turtle, for that matter) can use this trick. One giant tortoise reaches a weight of more than five hundred pounds, and formerly thrived on tiny islands north of Madagascar. It has suffered at the hands of man like the Galápagos tortoises. Now it is in a state of semidomestication on the Seychelles, but is still free-living on Aldabra. Madagascar and the mainland of Africa also have large species, some of them with brightly colored shells.

The true chameleons are perhaps the only African and Madagascan lizards that we hear about in the New World. Why have they so completely stolen the show when no fewer than ten other families occur in Africa and on Madagascar? Probably because these grotesque little creatures are the clowns among lizards. Their climbing habits and slow movements make their antics easy to watch. With the exception of two other small families, true chameleons make up the most representative of African and Madagascan lizard groups, very few species of true chameleons being found elsewhere. These few occur in Europe and Asia. The lizard known as "chameleon" in the United States is not even a close relative of the real thing. The early settlers called our anole "cha-

This Langaha snake of Madagascar has a truly remarkable proboscis.

The geometric tortoise (left) lives in southern Africa and has a beautiful yellow and black shell. The shields are raised like pyramids. This hinged-back tortoise (right), found in western Africa, can lower the hind part of the upper shell to fit against the lower one. A detail of this close fit is shown above the tortoise.

meleon" because it changes color. These people did not know that true chameleons are by no means the only lizards able to do this.

True chameleons vary in size, the smallest being less than two inches long, the largest over two feet. In shape they differ noticeably from species to species (of which there are more than eighty in all) but, nevertheless, they have an unmistakable look about them. When you first see one with, let us say, three horns, you might well wonder what right it has to be so odd. The body is flattened from side to side, making the animal seem to stand on edge; the adjective "popeyed" scarcely does it justice, and, to make matters worse, the great eyes often move in opposite directions at the same moment; the toes are bound in groups that give the feet tweezerlike action, and the tail curls about anything it happens to touch. But the chameleon has to be fed in order to show its best trick. An insect or spider is stalked by slow movements in strong contrast to those we usually associate with lizards. Then, when the prey is still far away, a tongue much longer than the lizard's head and body shoots out and, almost faster than the eye can see, laps up the prey. Now add to this the abilities to change color rapidly, to inflate as well as to flatten the body, and to hiss. What more could you want? The true chameleon moves slowly through a short life, the indication being that only two or three years separate hatching from death.

The remaining African lizards are almost too numerous to mention. Geckos come first with about one hundred and forty species; Madagascar has more than a third as many. Skinks come next (about fifty on Madagascar), and after them chameleons (about half the known species on Madagascar) and lacertids (none on Madagascar). The last are the lizards so common in Europe and Asia but unknown in the New World. The two specialties already mentioned are the girdle-tailed lizards and the gerrhosaurids (no simple English name). The lizards of these two groups are varied in form, and abound in southern Africa; the latter also live on Madagascar. Africa has a few monitors and some agamids; both of these groups are widely distributed because they include species at home in deserts as well as others that live in the rain forests. Neither monitor nor agamid is found on Madagascar. This brings us to the fact that lizards well illustrate that basic dissimilarity between animals of Africa and Madagascar. Only four of Africa's ten lizard families have species on that fascinating island. In turn, Madagascar has a few lizards unknown on Africa but abundant in the United States and other parts of the New World.

The snakes of Africa are far more familiar to us than are its lizards. Among the well-known kinds are pythons, mambas, cobras, vipers (including the famous puff adder), and the boomslang. All but the pythons are venomous, and even the larger pythons, because of their strength, must be classed among dangerous snakes. In spite of this, Africa has no unusual proportion of venomous snakes; its vast tropical regions with deserts, rain forests, and high mountains harbor one of the three great harmless snake faunas of the world. The other two, of course, are found in tropical America and southeastern Asia. In addition to pythons, hundreds of species of venomless snakes frequent Africa from one end to the other. These are so numerous that they must be left to the imagination. Suffice it to say that they are to be found burrowing in the ground, crawling on its surface, climbing through bushes and trees, and swimming in fresh waters.

Most people think of India when a cobra is mentioned, and are surprised to learn that Africa has three times as many species of cobras as does Asia. It is also helpful to recall that our own two coral snakes and the great array of venomous Australian snakes are relatives of the cobras. African cobras do not spread hoods as fancy as that of the Indian cobra, but they make up for this lack in other ways. Some of them, for instance, are "spitters" and squirt venom to a distance of several feet. This sounds more terrifying than it actually is. The venom has to get into the human eye to do harm, and, even there, if promptly washed out, may cause only severe pain. A snake hunter with any sort of eye protection is perfectly safe. Moreover, it is far better to be spat at than to be bitten. A cobra could scarcely get its prey by spitting, so it is hard to see why this habit developed. Possibly it is most useful when the enemy is a hoofed mammal that can trample the snake to death without being harmed by the fang, which is short. A few African cobras have even taken to the waters of lakes and rivers, where they feed on fishes.

The most fear-inspiring snake of Africa is the black mamba, a slender relative of the cobras. It reaches a length of fourteen feet. This snake has been hopelessly confused with the green mamba, a much smaller and less dangerous cousin. The trouble is that both are green when young; the big species turns brown or almost black with growth. Mambas raise the head and forebody when fighting. As a matter of fact, even the black mamba prefers to retreat, attacking only when pressed by an enemy. Mambas climb. Suddenly coming upon one at eye level is, of course, terrifying for anyone who fears snakes.

The snakes of Madagascar are quite different from those of Africa. Africa has several pythons and many venomous snakes; Madagascar has neither. Madagascar has boas; southern Africa lacks these, and the only boas of central and northern Africa are distant relatives of Madagascar's boas, which are like those of the New World.

The real oddities among Madagascan snakes are two species with noses extended into a proboscis almost as long as the head proper. In males, the proboscis is smoothly scaled and pointed; in females, its scales flare out, making the proboscis look like a scaly bulb. The use of this appendage remains a mystery because the habits of these Langaha snakes have not been studied.

Australia, New Guinea, and New Zealand

ANYONE looking at a map might guess from the position of Australia that it has unusual animals, and so it has. How the marsupials (animals—such as the kangaroos—having a pouch for carrying the young) got there early and took over is a fascinating story often told. Isolation was the key to their success; they never could have held out against many of the aggressive meat-eaters (carnivores) that swarmed in other parts of the world. Although the Australian reptiles cannot compare in out-landishness, they do have distinction.

Before taking up the reptiles in detail, let us look at Australia itself. Besides being the only one of our six areas not close to or connected with another, this island con-tinent is considerably the smallest of the six, and even slightly smaller than the United States. Its location straddling the Tropic of Capricorn gives it a variety of climates. Although its highest elevations are only com-parable in height to our eastern mountains, the great central desert of Australia is more extensive than the warm deserts of North America. There is difference of opinion as to the length of time that Australia has been an island; probably it has been one for many tens of millions of years. This has given the reptiles of every group plenty of time to develop many species very different from those found on other continents.

Australia has a reasonable share of the twenty-three crocodilians of the world: the salt-water and the Australian crocodiles. The former is the wide-ranging giant that grows to be twenty feet long, the latter, a slender-snouted species never more than eight feet in length. Both of these occur in extreme northern Australia where the bigger one is confined to the coasts.

All of the nonmarine turtles of Australia are snake-necked turtles; they belong to a family found only in Australia, New Guinea, and South America. I have already explained how the head of these odd reptiles is turned to one side to be hidden under the edge of the shell. Fourteen species, or nearly half of all known kinds, are found in Australia, and these fourteen vary considerably in appearance. One of them, sometimes called the Australian long-necked turtle, can be seen in many zoos. It is a docile animal with a bite so weak that it can be called little more than a nip. The turtles of this island continent are, then, truly unusual; only in South America and New Guinea can one find somewhat similar reptiles.

Many remarkable lizards are found in Australia, yet it must be admitted that no one group is peculiar to that island continent. In fact, two of its five families are

EAST INDIAN ISLANDS

NEW GUINEA

A U S T R A L I A

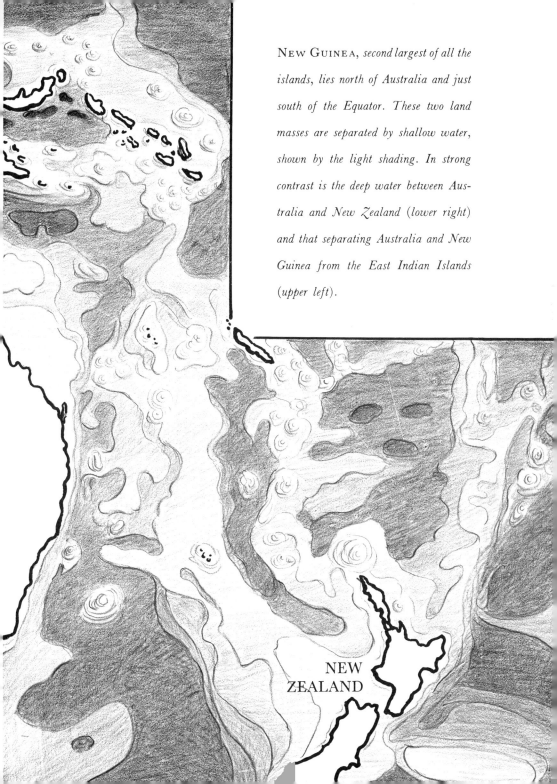

NEW GUINEA, *second largest of all the islands, lies north of Australia and just south of the Equator. These two land masses are separated by shallow water, shown by the light shading. In strong contrast is the deep water between Australia and New Zealand (lower right) and that separating Australia and New Guinea from the East Indian Islands (upper left).*

NEW
ZEALAND

world-wide in distribution, and two others are found westward to Africa. The former are the skinks and the geckos, the latter the agamids and the monitors. The nearest to an Australian specialty is the family of snake-lizards; these are shared only with New Guinea. The snake-lizards are an odd lot composed of nearly twenty species, the great majority of which are Australian. There are no front limbs, and the hind ones are mere flaps; the tail is very long, and it is not surprising that they move like snakes. The eyelid is not movable; this makes them even more snakelike. The biggest kinds grow to be about two feet long.

So much for Australia's lizard specialty. Next we come to the skinks, the most abundant lot. In addition to a great number of what we might call ordinary skinks, Australia has several giants. These put all but one other skink to shame. Some grow to be about twenty inches long. The prize among them is the stump-tailed lizard or shingle-back, which has thick scales that noticeably overlap. The tail is shaped much like the stumpy head, and the creature is further noteworthy for giving birth rather than laying eggs; two young are born at a time. Shingle-backs become very tame and make fine pets.

Australia might well be called the land of monitors, since twelve, half of all living species, occur there. Now monitors, as you know, are *the* giants among lizards, but Australia, just to be different, has two tiny kinds only eight or ten inches long. The Komodo dragon, largest of all and sometimes ten feet long, may, as already stated, weigh some thirty-seven hundred times as much as one of these dwarfs. Though found throughout Australia, monitors do not inhabit Tasmania. A fair number of both agamids and geckos live in Australia. Some of the former are large and startling in appearance, though it is a little species that has special interest for us. This, the moloch, looks enough like one of our own horned toads to make you wonder how it got that way. It will help to recall that North America and Australia have great deserts; both horned toads and moloch are desert animals, but they are by no means close relatives. Here is a fine example of parallel evolution, two unrelated animals that developed a striking likeness presumably because they lived under similar conditions.

It is a matter of considerable interest that Australia, alone among all the continents, has many more venomous than harmless snakes. No other continent has nearly as many venomous as harmless species. In Europe, a little more than two-thirds of the species are harmless. In the United States, as already indicated, the harmless kinds outnumber the others roughly five to one.

Does this great proportion of venomous species make Australia a dangerous place for man? This is the question that first comes to mind, and the answer is negative. To begin with, the venomous snakes of Australia are a very special lot. All are either elapids or sea snakes, which means that they are relatives of our own coral snakes; no viper of any description is found in Australia. Coral snakes, as you know, have short, rigid fangs, and a habit of biting only at close range rather than striking out like vipers. Because of all this, a small coral snake, in spite of its venom, is not very dangerous. A great many of the Australian elapids are small, and almost never get their

venom into a human being. Sea snakes, which we may
think of as marine coral snakes, make up a fair proportion
of Australia's venomous species, and sea snakes bite
human beings even less frequently than do the small New
World coral snakes. This brings us to a paradox. Perhaps four-fifths of Australia's venomous serpents do little
or no harm to man. Nevertheless, the reptile student
must state that the great majority of Australian snakes
are dangerous; if he does not, some persons might take
chances with the sea snakes and small elapids. It is better
never to get close enough to one to step on it, let alone
pick it up.

I have just said that Australian venomous snakes are
special, but I still have to explain all that I mean by this.
You may have read how the marsupials of this continent
took on the form and habits of nonmarsupials of other
regions. There are, among others, doglike, molelike, ant-
eaterlike, and flying-squirrellike, marsupials. The last
are locally known as flying or gliding "opossums." The
elapids did much the same thing, if to a lesser degree.
There are, for example, chunky elapids that look and act
for all the world like vipers, others that have medium
builds, and still others that are long and slender. These,
needless to add, are the highly dangerous kinds that
strike viciously, bringing terror to many who encounter
them. The ferocious taipan reaches a length of from ten
to eleven feet. It is so active that the capture of one un-
injured is anything but easy even for the experienced.
The tiger snake, the black snake, and the brown snake
all grow to be six feet long. The death adder, though
smaller, has the nasty habit of holding on when it bites.

In all continents except Australia the great majority of snake species are colubrids; in Australia only a few members of this array are found, and these live chiefly in the northern parts. Odds and ends of pythons occur in about the same number of species, and one of them, the amethystine python, reaches the respectable length of twenty-one feet. Worm- or blind snakes are somewhat more numerous than either of the foregoing groups. Here ends the list of the snakes of Australia. Its species are approximately equal in number to those of the United States. This is not surprising when we consider location, and recall that Australia and continental United States are about equal in size.

Next let us consider New Guinea, which lies just north of Australia and is often confused with the Guianas of northeastern South America. New Guinea, second largest island on earth, is almost as large as Texas and Louisiana combined. The northern part is within a hair's breadth of the Equator, and all of the island lies well within the tropics. Though much of it is low, a range of big mountains divides it lengthwise, the highest peak rising to an altitude of 16,400 feet, or nineteen hundred feet above our pride, Mount Whitney. If the sea level fell a mere hundred feet, New Guinea would again be connected with the tip of Australia, only a hundred miles away. To the geologist, New Guinea and Australia, only yesterday, were part of one land mass. Deep as well as shallow seas lie to the west of New Guinea, and these are studded with islands of many sizes. Beyond the deep seas, lie the great East Indian Islands.

What does all this lead you to expect of the reptiles of

New Guinea? First, they should be numerous and varied because of the tropical location and the great range of altitude. Second, they must be related to those of Australia as well as to those of the East Indian Islands. In spite of the deep seas separating New Guinea from the latter, the numerous islands in those seas made fine stepping-stones for reptiles able to do a reasonable amount of what is aptly called "island hopping."

Let us quickly consider some other reptiles found on this unique island. New Guinea has no crocodile all its own. One of its two species, the huge salt-water crocodile, is found all over that part of the world, the other, the New Guinea crocodile, in the Philippine Islands as well.

Twelve species of nonmarine turtles live on New Guinea, one of which is also found in the East Indian Islands, and four others in Australia and in New Guinea. This leaves seven for New Guinea alone. As to lizards, we find abundant in New Guinea the same three families of wide distribution that are common in Australia as well as in the East Indian Islands. These are geckos, agamids, and skinks. When it comes to lizard oddities, there is little to choose between New Guinea and Australia. New Guinea shares with Australia alone those peculiar creatures known as snake-lizards, and with the East Indian Islands and southeastern Asia the even more peculiar dibamids. These wormlike lizards must be blind; the eyes are under the scales. In doing away with limbs, they have gone even further than the snake-lizards. Only the males have any limbs, and these, a single pair, are tiny flaps.

Like Australia, New Guinea has no vipers. The outstanding thing about the snakes of New Guinea in comparison with those of Australia is this: in Australia, coral snake relatives (the elapids) comprise the majority of all snakes, whereas in New Guinea, they are a mere fraction of the whole snake fauna though roughly equal in number to the colubrid element. In New Guinea, and nowhere else on earth, these two groups have nearly hit a balance. On New Guinea, then, one finds a grand mixture of reptiles, a goodly share of specialties well diluted with elements from both Australia and the East Indian Islands.

New Zealand lies some twelve hundred miles southeast of Australia, and is only a third the size of New Guinea. No other large island of the temperate and tropical parts of the world is so remote. The center of New Zealand is about as far south of the Equator as New York City is north of it. It would hardly be fair to ask you to guess what animals were once found on this distant island. I say "were once found" because man has brought about great changes in comparatively recent times.

There were no walking land mammals but there were plenty of birds, many of them very odd. Only two amphibians lived there in the past, and they still do; both of them are strange frogs whose closest relatives are found in western North America. Leaving out of consideration wide-ranging marine reptiles (sea snakes and sea turtles), New Zealand has neither crocodilian, snake, nor turtle, and only a few species of lizards (geckos and skinks) plus the one grand surprise, the tuatara. This "living fossil" has already been mentioned in the chapter on ancient reptiles. If you are ever lucky enough to see one of the few tuataras in our zoos, remember that it is every bit as extraordinary as a lone dinosaur would be.

Common and Technical Names

of Species and Genera in this Book

SCIENTISTS of all parts of the world use the same technical names of animals. Without these, progress in zoology would be extremely slow and laborious. As a means of world-wide communication, such standard names should command great respect. The difficulty of learning them is nothing in comparison with the necessity of having them

Unfortunately, common names for the reptiles of the world have never been standardized even in English, let alone in any other of the hundreds of important languages. Only recently has the American Society of Ichthyologists and Herpetologists published a list for the layman: "Common Names for North American Amphibians and Reptiles."* With few exceptions, I have used the names of this list. These exceptions have been indicated in the text.

Copeia, 1956, No. 3, pp. 172–185. Also available in amplified form as a separate publication. Copies of either this *Copeia* or the amplified list can be obtained from Professor N. B. Green, Biology Department, Marshall College, Huntington, West Virginia.

CROCODILIANS
(Order *Crocodilia*)

TRUE CROCODILES

African Slender-snouted Crocodile	*Crocodylus cataphractus*
American Crocodile	*Crocodylus acutus*
Australian Crocodile	*Crocodylus johnsoni*
Cuban Crocodile	*Crocodylus rhombifer*
Mugger or Marsh Crocodile	*Crocodylus palustris*
New Guinea Crocodile	*Crocodylus novæ-guineæ*
Nile Crocodile	*Crocodylus niloticus*
Orinoco Crocodile	*Crocodylus intermedius*
Salt-water Crocodile	*Crocodylus porosus*

OTHER CROCODILIANS

American Alligator	*Alligator mississippiensis*
Black Caiman	*Melanosuchus niger*
Chinese Alligator	*Alligator sinensis*
Congo Dwarf Crocodile	*Osteolæmus osborni*
False Gavial	*Tomistoma schlegeli*
Gavial or Gharial	*Gavialis gangeticus*
Spectacled Caiman	*Caiman sclerops*

TURTLES
(Order *Chelonia*)

SNAPPING TURTLES (Chelydridæ)

Alligator Snapping Turtle	*Macrochelys temmincki*
Snapping Turtle	*Chelydra serpentina*

FRESH-WATER TURTLES OR EMYDIDS (Emydidæ)

Bog Turtle	*Clemmys muhlenbergi*
Box Turtle	*Terrapene carolina*
Box Turtles	*Terrapene* (genus)
Cooter	*Pseudemys floridana*

Diamondback Terrapin	*Malaclemys terrapin*
Eastern Box Turtle	*Terrapene carolina*
Painted Turtle	*Chrysemys picta*
Western Pond Turtle	*Clemmys marmorata*
Wood Turtle	*Clemmys insculpta*

TRUE TORTOISES (Testudinidæ)

Desert Tortoise	*Gopherus agassizi*
Geometric Tortoise	*Testudo geometrica*
Giant Tortoises	*Testudo* (genus, part)
Gopher Tortoise	*Gopherus polyphemus*
Hinged-back Tortoise	*Kinixys erosa*
South American Tortoise	*Testudo denticulata*
Texas Tortoise	*Gopherus berlandieri*

SEA TURTLES (Cheloniidæ)

Green Turtle	*Chelonia mydas*
Hawksbill	*Eretmochelys imbricata*
Leatherback	*Dermochelys coriacea*
Loggerhead	*Caretta caretta*

OTHER TURTLES

Australian Long-necked Turtle	*Chelodina longicollis*
Big-headed Turtle	*Platysternon megacephalum*
Mud Turtles	*Kinosternon* (genus)
Musk Turtles	*Sternotherus* (genus)
Softshell Turtles	*Trionyx* (and other genera)
Yellow Mud Turtle	*Kinosternon flavescens*

LIZARDS
(Suborder *Sauria*)

IGUANAS OR IGUANIDS (Iguanidæ)

American Chameleon or Carolina Anole	*Anolis carolinensis*
Anoles	*Anolis* (genus)

Black Iguana	*Acanthosaura pectinata*
Chuckwalla	*Sauromalus obesus*
Collared Lizard	*Crotaphytus collaris*
Common Iguana	*Iguana iguana*
Earless Lizards	*Holbrookia* (genus)
Fringe-toed Lizard	*Uma notata*
Horned Toads or Horned Lizards	*Phrynosoma* (genus)
Leopard Lizard	*Crotaphytus wislizeni*
Marine Iguana	*Amblyrhynchus cristatus*
Spiny Lizards or Swifts	*Sceloporus* (genus)
Utas	*Uta* (genus)

SKINKS (Scincidæ)

Five-lined Skink	*Eumeces fasciatus*
Sand Skink	*Neoseps reynoldsi*
Shingle-back or Stump-tailed Lizard	*Trachysaurus rugosus*

TEIIDS (Teiidæ)

Caiman Lizard	*Dracæna guianensis*
Dwarf Spiny Lizard	*Leposoma percarinatum*
Northern Tegu	*Tupinambis nigropunctatus*
Racerunner	*Cnemidophorus sexlineatus*
Tegus	*Tupinambis* (genus)
Whiptails	*Cnemidophorus* (genus, part)

OTHER LIZARDS

Alligator Lizards	*Gerrhonotus* (genus)
European Glass Snake	*Ophisaurus apodus*
Flying Dragons	*Draco* (genus)
Gerrhosaurids	*Gerrhosaurus* (and other genera)
Gila Monster	*Heloderma suspectum*
Girdle-tailed Lizards	*Cordylus* (and other genera)
Glass Snakes or Glass Lizards	*Ophisaurus* (genus)
Komodo Dragon	*Varanus komodoensis*
Mexican Beaded Lizard	*Heloderma horridum*

Moloch	*Moloch horridus*
Monitors	*Varanus* (genus)
Slow-worm	*Anguis fragilis*
True Chameleons	*Chamæleo* (and other genera)

SNAKES
(Suborder *Serpentes*)

BOAS AND PYTHONS (Boidæ)

Amethystine Python	*Python amethistinus*
Anaconda	*Eunectes murinus*
Australian Black-headed Python	*Aspidites melanocephalus*
Boa Constrictor	*Boa constrictor*
Indian Python	*Python molurus*
Rainbow Boa	*Epicrates cenchris*
Reticulate Python	*Python reticulatus*
Rock Python	*Python sebæ*
Rosy Boa	*Lichanura roseofusca*
Rubber Boa	*Charina bottæ*
Sand Boas	*Eryx* (genus)

COLUBRID SNAKES (Colubridæ)

Æsculapius Snake	*Elaphe longissima*
Boomslang	*Dispholidus typus*
Bullsnakes	*Pituophis* (genus)
Common Garter Snake	*Thamnophis sirtalis*
Egg-eating Snake	*Dasypeltis scaber*
Garter Snakes	*Thamnophis* (genus)
Hognose Snakes	*Heterodon* (genus)
Kingsnakes	*Lampropeltis* (genus)
Langaha Snakes	*Langaha* (genus)
Milk Snake	*Lampropeltis doliata*
Racers	*Coluber* (genus)
Rat Snakes	*Elaphe* (genus)
Tree Snake	*Oxybelis* (species of)
Wart Snakes	*Acrochordus* (genus)

Water Snakes	*Natrix* (genus)
Whipsnakes	*Masticophis* (genus)

COBRAS, CORAL SNAKES, AND ALLIES; ELAPIDS (Elapidæ)

Arizona Coral Snake	*Micruroides euryxanthus*
Australian Black Snake	*Pseudechis porphyriacus*
Australian Brown Snake	*Demansia textilis*
Black Mamba	*Dendroaspis polylepis*
Death Adder	*Acanthophis antarcticus*
Eastern Coral Snake	*Micrurus fulvius*
Green Mamba	*Dendroaspis angusticeps*
Indian Cobra	*Naja naja*
King Cobra	*Ophiophagus hannah*
Mambas	*Dendroaspis* (genus)
Taipan	*Oxyuranus scutellatus*
Tiger Snake	*Notechis scutatus*

SEA SNAKES (Hydrophiidæ)

Yellow-bellied Sea Snake	*Pelamis platurus*

VIPERS (Viperidæ)

Bushmaster	*Lachesis muta*
Canebrake Rattlesnake	*Crotalus horridus*
Cascabel or Tropical Rattlesnake	*Crotalus durissus*
Copperhead	*Ancistrodon contortrix*
Cottonmouth or Water Moccasin	*Ancistrodon piscivorus*
Fer-de-lance	*Bothrops atrox*
Gaboon Viper	*Bitis gabonica*
Massasauga	*Sistrurus catenatus*
Mexican Cottonmouth	*Ancistrodon bilineatus*
Prairie Rattlesnake	*Crotalus viridis*
Puff Adder	*Bitis lachesis*
Rattlesnakes	*Crotalus* and *Sistrurus* (genera)
Sidewinder	*Crotalus cerastes*

Index

CLIFFORD H. POPE, who was born in Georgia, is well known both in this country and abroad as a distinguished herpetologist. A past president of the American Society of Ichthyologists and Herpetologists, he has also served as Assistant Curator of Herpetology at The American Museum of Natural History and as Curator of the Division of Amphibians and Reptiles at Chicago Natural History Museum. Mr. Pope spent four years in China with the Central Asiatic Expeditions led by Roy Chapman Andrews, and has himself led many other scientific expeditions in Mexico and the United States. He now lives with his wife in Winnetka, Illinois, and is the father of three sons. Among his best known works are *The Reptile World, Snakes Alive and How They Live*, and *Turtles of the United States and Canada*.

HELEN DAMROSCH TEE-VAN, a native of New York City, is recognized as an expert illustrator of undersea life, animals, and flowers. She has been the artist on numerous expeditions of the Tropical Research Department of the New York Zoological Society under the direction of William Beebe. Besides having done illustrations for the *Encyclopædia Britannica, Collier's Encyclopedia*, and scientific publications, Mrs. Tee-Van has painted murals for the Bronx Zoo and the Berkshire Museum in Pittsfield, Massachusetts. Her work has been exhibited at the Metropolitan Museum and The American Museum of Natural History in New York. She is the wife of Dr. John Tee-Van, Director of the New York Zoological Park and Aquarium.